T0129902

LATE
DECLARED
SON

JACQUES SIMON

authorHOUSE®

AuthorHouse™
1663 Liberty Drive
Bloomington, IN 47403
www.authorhouse.com
Phone: 1 (800) 839-8640

Published by AuthorHouse   11/09/2015

ISBN: 978-1-5049-5860-8 (sc)
ISBN: 978-1-5049-5862-2 (hc)
ISBN: 978-1-5049-5861-5 (e)

Library of Congress Control Number: 2015917819

Print information available on the last page.

To my Wife
Marie-Banatte Simon

To my Children
Jadesara Bajemar Simon
Janeseey Bajemar Simon
Jeremiah Jadeson Simon

To my Mother
Mme Elmalite Simon

To my Brothers and Sisters
Marc-Antoine Simon
Paulette Verpile
David Simon
Josué Simon
Decimus Simon
Michel Simon

FOREWORD ....

Nowadays, on a daily basis, we use terms such as "blended family", "single parent", "mother-centered family", "foster care", and "parental abandonment and resignation" to describe various aspects of the family life. However, as long as the global situation deteriorates, especially we see the number of teenage mothers and adult-single parents increase. Wars primarily fatal to men, the skyrocketing divorce rate everywhere, and the moral decay of our era are among the causes of that crisis incompatible with the family happiness. It is undeniable that children should be the ones to pay the consequences in our society!

In many countries, a lot of these "fatherless children" go across deprivation and poverty. Living only at the expenses of their brave mothers, they often feel a void in their life. In fact, many of them are as miserable as they are shown in the media: desperate, starving, homeless, plagued by illness, exposed to domesticity or slavery, subject to kidnapping, to juvenile delinquency and even to prostitution! Despite all, their ordeal would be worse without their Father in the heaven to end their various situations at any time! This dark reality affecting those unfortunate children throughout earth also echoes in this tale entitled "*Late Declared Son.*"

There is no doubt that the readers of this poetic tale will grow in the love of the mothers and of the children around the World while admiring particularly this who dominates this storyline from start to end. May this work please to everyone!

Dedicated to Yvon Montes

Look at my "*Late Declared Son*" wailing in his crib!
He hankers after you for warmly hugging him!
Poet, he needs your love and your great compassion!
Oh! Please, examine him from his opening verse
To the one having closed his narrative pages!
Oh! How he will prize your wise criticism!
A boy whose existence had looked like a shipwreck,
Friend, it is the backdrop of this poetic work!
And I have called him Jain. I wish he could charm you!
"Fatherless" he only had one trick up his sleeves.
At the very moment of his woes, however,
He ended up to feeding a strong optimism
Although his mother then going round the World
Left him to face alone all his cruel sufferings.
For now, you a poet and a father who love
All the boys and the girls cheering their parents up,
Please, appreciate of Jain the filial piety!
In the same vein, may you consider, O writer,
The foolish decisions of his regretful mom!
And of his stepfather look at the blind passion,
At the ups and the downs and at the right anger!
Deign to ponder over the so worthy courage
Which others will display in the time of peril
Even when a horrible surprise should daze them!
Apart from the factors regarding those actors,
Fell free, Friend, to enjoy their pleasant sightseeing
While they thrive to lead a so profligate life
Anywhere their journey will lead them in the plot!
Delight with them in the nocturnal orchestra
Of tropical insects at autumnal darkness!
And let the glittering ether catch your both eyes
As the stars' light adorns the jovial firmament!

Take a seat among them aboard the splendid ship
For a tour to sites once centers of nice things!
Go from Acapulco to the Italian soil,
From Venice to Athens, from Athens to Egypt!
And then check the facts which all our classic teachers
Told us of the Aztecs and of other nations
When it came to learning their civilization!
Follow your companions to the Black Africa
Of which footprints we keep deeply in memory!
And come back with them, please, after so happy days!
Then, you will forget those whom you leave in Europe,
I mean, those journeyers, who fell into distress,
Because as they left you, they felt their "Calvary",
While your men and you said goodbye in Cairo!
Then you too, come back, please, with your people to Jain,
To that abandoned son, he who had been nowhere!
And then you'll come back as a safe eyewitness
Of the lessons which all sincere hearts should accept!
And the end will tell you it's a story to read,
An artwork containing the cure for all people
Regardless of their race and nationality
While going across fearsome calamities!
A poem addressing readers of all ages,
To remind all of them of the need to be wise
And to avoid well-unsuccessful decisions,
So they can all enjoy a lasting well-being.

Jacques Simon
Late Declared Son

CHAPTER ONE

The Tears of Jain

If a torrent of tears is streaming from your eyes
So much so you submerge your city in your drops,
Keep yourself from thinking you are the only one
To wail over yours grief and your atrocities!
For I saw a young man who just turned twelve years old
Bursting into tears on account of his mom!
Had he lost his mother at that very moment?
Or did anything else cause him to lament her?
"Would you mind telling me why you're weeping, my man?"
I asked the tearful guy with commiseration!
Then he took a while to answer my question.
"How can I empathize with your moaning, O boy?
And root out of your heart these thorns and brambles?"
Before my persistence, he felt all-decided
On unloading on me his deepest emotion
"Ah, Sir, sometimes," he said, "I find my life worthless!"
"Maybe, crying that much, I look like a drunkard!
However, I would like my long lamentation
To tell you what has caused my bottomless sadness!
And then you will well know that my desolation
Has made me a unique-young man through my distress!

"My mother had just turned thirteen when I was born.
What a pity! What was the good reason for that?
On her bad company they blamed then her mistake.
Furious were her parents who saw in it a curse!
Worse yet, was my father a young man in the street,
A man without hope of becoming someone!
While my mother's class was in the public gaze!
No need to say how much they felt disappointed!
And at that time in my ancestral area

An out wedlock birth was a so shameful thing
That they sent my early mother live far away
And deprived her of me, her sad -new- first-born child!
Since then I was given my grandma for guardian
In this countryside where my mom never came
And where I grew up as a sad fatherless child!

In the meantime, my mom, in her urban district
Changed her image and resumed the journey to school!
She learned how to avoid all dangerous boyfriends
And how to stay away from risky misconducts!
And soon after getting her High school diploma,
She got trained as a health-care professional.
And she hardly had time to start her nice nurse job
That she had already found a kind suitor
Who belongs to a well known and rich family!
He really fell in love with my pretty mother!
And he was so ablaze with his passion for her
That he couldn't help taking her into marriage soon!
And then my mom, alas, refrained from telling him
Her having a young son in her countryside!
And on his part, the proud suitor would never think
That she would already breastfeed me, her poor boy!

At twenty-three years old in fact she got married.
At that time, however, I had never met her!
Nor felt I missing her when Grandma was alive!
I was always said that my mom lives somewhere
And that she would come back and get me any day!
I pined over that time in an endless ecstasy
In hope of experiencing her sweet affection!
Unhappily, one day my grandma fell ailing
And her illness took her to the cruel verge of death!
I saw a young lady entering the house,
Who had so many tears flowing from her both eyes!

And she warmly hugged me and gazed at me as well! 'Would this visitor
be my Mom?' I asked myself
While throwing me in her arms and watching her!
Oh, I experienced a time of supreme joy!

"She, my grandma, and I we were three in that room
In which Grandma watched my Mom's joy mingled with pain.
Then confined in her bed the sick ancestor told,
'Resign yourself to what you're seeing, Daughter!
I'm leaving you right now for my last dwelling!
Please take - your boy with you, tell him about all!
Tell him why in my hands you left him for so long!
Tell him why you had abandoned him here that much!
Let me go for I can no longer bear my pains.
And I hope your husband will get along with you
When you sincerely seek to get his forgiveness!
Try to confess to him in your early teenage,
Against your own willing you had conceived that boy!
And please, don't let me go before you promise me
You will take good care of my little beloved son
Whom I must leave, alas, for the place which calls me!
As for your two children, who live in the City,
And who have never met Jain their older brother,
Let them know without disturbing their young mind
In what circumstances you became Jain's mother.
Don't worry about me because I have to go.
I am ready for the funeral expenses.
My little boy will show you where to bury me.
Cheer up! Let God bless you! Become well successful!'

Thus had spoken Grandma to whom I have owed
To remain well alive since I was one year old!
And then she closed her eyes, and I felt run down
After she stopped breathing!
Oh! What a tragic pain to lose a loved one!
To lose someone who by her tender- kind presence

Had made me stay far from bitterness all the time!
And had instilled in me an ineffable joy!
I felt that suffering which tore my entire heart!
What a cruel trial when I saw my grandma
Say goodbye forever with an emaciated face!

So loudly we mourned then her sad passing away
That the whole neighborhood having heard our crying
Flocked to our mournful home to show their sympathy!
They all deplored our loss, which to speak bluntly,
Was unavoidable! For Grandma had to leave
Because her illness gave her the coup de grace
To hasten my torments!

They in whom death delights are often the best ones
Among all the mortals regardless of the time!
My affliction was worse to see her leaving us
When they took her remains to the funeral home,
Sounding the alarms which saddened the quarter!
And I felt my trouble getting worse in that day
As long as trough any vicinal path showed up
A sympathetic friend who had already known
That should go anytime the well-known ancestor,
Who was so worthy of regret and gratitude!"

CHAPTER TWO

Farewell, Grandma,

I kept quiet while listening to the sullen child.
Considering my silence as an expression of sympathy,
He continued to unburden on me his depths of despair,
Which he did through these pathetic words:

"Immediately, after Grandma died," Jain said,
"My mother dispatched a messenger to the City
To apprise her husband and her two other sons of that decease!
Meanwhile, she worked hard
In order to prepare their visit to the grieving house!
Then my grief got so worse, for in that circumstance,
She bid me to hide my filial relationship to her!
In fact, she feared that presenting me as her first-born child
Might hugely surprise the spouse and ruin her credibility as well!
The problem lies in the fact that before their engagement
She had talked so good about herself!
Anyway, I kept wondering whether that staging would be long lasting
Or if would I spend the rest of my life covering my true identity
By presenting me as my mom's cousin!
I am telling you! I did not feel like doing so!
How to resign myself to play this scenario
During this gloomy period when my grandmother just died?
Moreover, telling people I am not her son
Would increase my trouble in those days!
Despite all, when her family came to our house,
I strived to cooperate with her.
I did my best to assist her at these cruel times
In which the burial was approaching!
I did very well then by impersonating his cousin,
Which she had decided with a sovereign tone!
I gave her my whole entire support to preclude her embarrassment!

"Finally, the day that we expected arrived.
Everyone was ready to pay tribute
I mean, a last tribute to my defunct-grandmother,
To that ancestor whom everyone had seen as a wise woman!
This is the toughest time which a bereaved one might experience
When he must go to the graveyard and bid farewell to a beloved grandma,
And hear a final prayer in her memory!

And it's even worse when seeing the coffin
Smoothly slip into the little space
In which shall stay the one who put us in mourning
In a heavy grief such as it crushes our body parts
And removes the taste of food from our palate
And causes our blue sky to become so dark
That everything in existence loses it attractions and beauty
And that a countless number of negative ideas assail us!
This is what my grandmother left at her departure
After we accompanied her to the necropolis!

Since that test, I have felt so afflicted!
And my soul has fallen into loneliness!
And this is not, O Sir, the end of my sad story!"
Exclaimed the young man with a grieving face!

"My existence exposed to endless disappointments
Now, seems to be a shredded shrub!
It's like when winter approaches and that the vegetation
Strips of everything that makes its attractions:
Then its foliage losing its greenery gets yellowed,
And withers by the fact of a natural order!
Therefore, the shrub loses its foliage
And appears to be in destruction process
And sometimes, seems to be dead!
This is what I look like today,
I who have suffered so much loneliness!
I thought I could take leave of my distress!
And get a balm to my sorrows next to my mother!

Yet my sad life she made worse by increasing my pain and my cares!

"Alas! My true happiness had lasted an hour only,
The only one hour I spent crying in her arms
Under the eyes of my grandmother before she died of a quick death!
Since then, I can no longer hug my mother
Nor enjoy her caress, nor comfort me next to her
And her indifference has embittered me
So that I really see myself like an alienated child!

As soon as Grandma was buried, my mother folded luggage
So she and her people could go back to their city home.
And as she got ready to take her leave,
She spoke of returning soon, but just to calm me down!
However, I was still playing my role as little cousin as wanted;
I did it so perfectly well in this drama!
Until came that sad morning for me to witness her departure!

Upset I tried with tact, but in vain, to convince her to stay longer
So her presence could comfort me or help my soul overcome my desolation!
At this time, she invited me to a separate room and tried to coax me as follows:

'Thank you, Son, for covering the truth!' She told me, at that time.
'O Son, how mad should have you been at me!
Since I had you dissimulate the fact that you are my son!
However, If you see my behaving
As if no affective link existed between you and me,
It does never follow that I wanted to humiliate you!
I did so because I feared that my husband discovering the truth
Might grow indignant and stop seeing me
As the most credible wife that has ever existed in his eyes!
Oh, absolve me of this serious lie!
I have questioned myself since the day I had left you!'
So Linda had whispered to her son Jain.
Then I seized the opportunity to tell her about my cares."

CHAPTER THREE

Who else will love me?

Then the young man fearlessly spoke to me
So he could unload his heart of his flooding laments.
And since I realized that he was looking for some comfort,
I paid close attention to his grievances,
Which I thought could relieve him.
Then he exposed to me every single thing he had told his mother as follows

"O Mom, how come have you spoiled your other sons and abandoned me?
Am I not your first- born child?" He said.
"Am I not like them the fruit of your womb?
Every single day! You have nurtured them!
And you have sent nothing to me! Not even ten cents?
Since the dark hour at which you turned your back to me
Up to the current time, nothing you have sent to me!
Ah! What crime did I make! Tell me, Mom!
Tell me what crime I committed by coming to Earth
So I should lose the right, oh, the same right as my brothers!
You are going to abandon me like a child in the streets
To beg my bread and to sleep under the bridges!
You are going to deny me like a stranger,
To deny me, your first-born child, in the eyes of the heaven!
Really! You are going to deny me
As you have done to the man who put me on Earth!
The man whose name sounded, wrongly or rightly, as an infamy
At my grandmother's ears!
What will happen to me when you just leave me after the funeral?
What is your dream for me since you want to leave now?
And I will feel alone wherever I should go!
And who else will love me for real?
Will I not feel lonely next to them, the people with whom you entrust my
life?
Will they treat me with empathy and sincerity?

And shall I earn my daily bread working as a child in domestic service?
Like these parentless slaves abused by their merciless masters!
Since you forsake me, is it indeed the hardship
That I shall embrace as do now many orphans like me?
As do now these children whom hunger bites, o God,
Without someone to hear their Paternosters under their domestic yoke!
Where they get up early and go to bed very late!
Where they work in two places at once!
For the welfare of their masters' children
The only ones children to bank on school for their future!
No! Putting children in domestic services is not a bad thing, Mother!
But their welfare depends on the good treatments which they receive!
Otherwise, it's a boy in slavery!
A girl dedicated to painful purposes!
A toddler beat-up with rage!
Or punished for a peccadillo without pity and with disdain!
Is that what awaits my poor soul, Mom,
After my grandmother going to her ancestors
Made you swear in the name of God
That you would take care of me?
Since you leave this morning, how many years yet
Before you back will have to elapse?
When the desire to see you, o mom, devours me,
Where therefore will I go and seek you? Tell me, please!'

At these words, the husband headed for the room where we were talking.
Upon hearing his drawing close to us,
I kept silent for the sake of my disturbed mother
Who then feigned to be in good mood!
And her husband entering the room could realize
That nothing suspicious was going on between us!
Then, I saw him hugging his wife with a marital caress
Whereas resuming my role of cousin, I left them alone inside!

But I vainly thought that she was touched enough to postpone her departure!

Despite the fires which my speech ignited in her maternal heart,
She took my complaints like a fairytale!
So she kept her decision on going home the same day.
She, her husband, and my two indifferent brothers took their leave.
Here me all-alone, which I had feared!
Here me alone, like this coffin that locked-up my grandmother!
Here me alone! In this house, without joy and merriment!
Here me alone! Losing a happiness which was only ephemeral!
I lost my case! And if that man did not marry her, I think,
You never know, considering my age, my mom would take pity on me!
She would support me until I grow to a mature man!"

Thus had spoken the sad and hopeless child!
Then no one could cure these staggering blows
That came to empoison his life!
He had too much on his plate
Since he was bereft of the one who was given him as Mom!
He had too much on his plate by turning that dark page!
He had too much on his plate when his own mother,
Instead of comforting his heart, denied him!
He had too much on his plate
When she presented him as cousin and sickened him that way!
And above all, he had too much in his plate
When he found himself so abandoned so early!

If the one owing you affection and love
Neglects you, denies you, or puts you in disgrace,
You can even think that death
Will finally conquer you, no matter the effort you make!

CHAPTER FOUR

A Child Exposed to Loneliness

For the first time at the falling night,
Jain realized that he was alone on Earth.
Tired of all and cast down,
He threw himself to a solitary corner and then slept around the clock.
Immersed and wrapped in a dream sleep,
He missed in that occasion the fantastic-constellated sky
To which the admirers of the azure vault clung their look!
He also missed the spectacle of twinkling stars in the Zenith
After the solar furnace
Having sunk itself into the sea had the night resume its trial!
And after it had made the firmament change gradually its appearance!

Jain was well and truly asleep
Whereas the stars were already lit as if by an invisible finger!
He was well and truly asleep
Whereas the stars hung-up in plethora in the infinite space
Like a swarm of multicolor points
That an artist would brilliantly embroider in a canvas!
He was well and truly asleep!

Maybe did sleep in its dreamlike phase
Make him contemplate in a Freudian scene
The ineffable universe with its poetic charms and attractions,
Which usually dispels every one's cares,
May be did Jain in his dreams solve all his problems
Given that sleep is a gift from our loving God
And a secret for any dejected one who needs to experience a happier day!

Alas! At that night,
The grieving boy ignored the wonderful- sidereal world!
He ignored this sphere which raises every poet to the pinnacle of his inspiration.

Alas! He also turned down the bucolic merriment
Which the night time provides to the country-side dwellers:
For as soon as the blue sky get embroidered with stars,
The anoles started their invisible concert!
And as soon as the zephyr drove any clouds away,
The nocturnal birds patrolled the ether!
And the fireflies exhibited their lights in the fields,
Flying from grassland to grassland in any directions,
Posing on branches, on tops of the cottages
Until the daylight taking over its throne extinguished their fire!

The night was quiet. Then, the braying of the foals
Ripped its silence like a clock!
Then the kittens in rut at the entrance to houses,
Purring of eroticism departed from this peace!
In the meantime, assuming their role of sentinels,
The dogs with tireless and irate barks
Denounced the passage of the usual queues of *maroulés*[1]
With several pairs of oxen toward Port-au-Prince!

And the song of the cock which dominates the night,
Either closely as from afar, or across resonated!
Yet did not such echo harm to anyone
Or disturb anyone whom sleep conquered.
Soon the night alternated with the daylight!
The rising sun dispersed the shadows!
And the constellations disappeared in turn!
And the solar rays reflected on the countless hills.
They beamed down on the heights of Desjardin[2] and the Mount Plato[3].
And once more, Chantal[4] Commune waked up

---

[1] This word should be pronounced like *mah-roo-lay* in English. The *maroulé* is the
    pedestrian peasant who walked oxen from a rural area market to Port-au-Prince
    (Haiti).
[2] This mount is located in the west of Chantal.
[3] The heights of Plato make part in the Massif de la Hotte that dominates the
    southwest part of Haiti.
[4] A commune in the arrondissement of Cayes.

Late Declared Son

As under a gentle breeze, the foliage whispered!
And the diurnal birds of prey came into scenes and feasted!
Then the tremolo of the jovial nightingale,
Tickling everyone's ears inspired joy!
Then Jain refreshed after a long sleep waked- up too!

He had taken a break from the beautiful nature for one night only!
He had just sought in sleep a relief from his distress!
Now he went back to the nature that put his heart in ecstasy
So he could overcome his loneliness!
For now on, his only one friend was found to be his maternal uncle.
This avuncular guardian undertook to walk him in the hinterland
Through the verdant plains,
Where they could together breathe at full breath in the wood!
The uncle considered doing that in order to appease the mournful nephew.
Then they were heading for *Madan Blaise*[5] which near Chantal City
Bewitched the passers-by!
There, between two hills, the boy was filled with joy
By the avian chirps emitted from a pond.
Oh! How beautiful was this valley!
When people from a hill admired its swarming with agricultural activities!

On the one hand, drunk chore men tilled the ground with concurrent hoe shots,
Howling, making a din, and asking for cold water or for a grog!
As sounded the tambourine of the head
Who to stimulate them kept drumming and singing at once!
Then someone was there to bring anything they were asking for
Until they were done with the whole task!

Finally, the landlord thanked these strong laborers
For coming from afar to plow his ground with force and energy!
And for honoring their contract in all respects!

---

[5]   Madan Blaise is a rustic area near Chantal City.

13

In fact, so early these valiant ploughmen had got up at the sound of a conch shell[6]
And had gathered from different places
So they could get to the labor together
And start working side-by-side as a good team!

On the other hand, ripen rice fields exposed to avian invasions awaited harvest.
Since the beginning of the green grains set,
Legions of birds took over the entire region everyday!
Therefore if the landlords left the fields unattended,
If they failed to build several statues of straws across them,
Nothing of the crop they would get!
For the raids of avian throngs into the garden
Would strip them of everything and drive them crazy!

As for Jain, he felt appeased by observing that pastoral scene!
And he remained despite all with a nostalgic face
Because he still was thinking about his absent mother.

---

[6]   In that countryside, the conch cell was used as a high-echoing-rallying instrument.

CHAPTER FIVE

Jain Looking for His Mother

Two years later, Linda never came back to her son
Who was sinking into a deep sadness!
However by a morning, after the young man stumbled into her address,
He ached for visiting her to the capital city, where she lived.
Then he persuaded his uncle to go with him,

"Uncle, since my mom left me two years ago," he said,
"I have been looking forward to seeing her!
Today, I can no longer bear my grief
After I accidentally discovered her address!
Please, would you mind dropping me at her house?"

Having heard that question, the avuncular guardian kept silent.
He looked at the nephew with bewilderment.
Nevertheless, the young man insisted,

"We will come back quickly, Uncle!
As soon as I quench my longing for seeing her,
Of course, we will come back!"

At first, the silent-parental guardian hesitated to do so.
But a while later, considering the profound distress of the boy,
He accepted to drop him at his mother's house.
No matter how mad he thought his careless sister would be at him.

Both uncle and nephew would got early to Chantal Commune, whence
They would go to Linda's house on board the *Belle Gitane* autobus.
It was Friday, the market day of that province.
Visitors and vacationers from everywhere flocked to that location!
And they felt at home whenever they came there,
For not only did the mayor of that administrative division welcome them
warmly,

He also ensured that all people were safe and secure!
In fact, the hospitable official enjoyed the presence of the outsiders.
Thus from time to time,
One might see many unknown ones swim in *l'Acul*[7]
Whose water was found to be always pristine!

In the meantime, at the Bador Restaurant near the station,
Jain and his uncle enjoyed their delicious breakfast.
After that, the young man had a good time before leaving for the capital City.
He got fun seeing one bag carrier juggling with a burden good for ten strong men!
He heard from the back yard of Chantal's market
The strident cries of the falling pigs slaughtered
By the ruthless knives of the butchers!

In that place also, the pig killers having killed the quadrupeds
Removed their hair and burned their skin with flaming branches!
Jain also heard the regular beats falling on slaughtered-swelling beefs
Of which blood was given to gluttonous dogs in the wait.

A while later both Jain and his uncle had to take their leave from the commune.
By the time, itinerant vendors cried out their hot snacks all over the place!
Visitors and buyers rushed into anything in retail or wholesale.
They paced back and forth. It's a special day!
Businessmen and merchants of grains,
Hardware sellers, traders of any products came there to make money!
And they relied on buyers coming from the vicinal places to do so
Wherever they came from: from Duclair or from Paulduc[8],
The traders relied on those clients!

At the entrance to the Chantal some speculators installed their scales
And expected to buy prodigal bags of coffee

---

[7] The largest river that waters Chantal.
[8] Duclair and Paulduc two rural sections in Chantal.

16

Which the peasants carried on burden beast back, from the neighboring
mounts!
Those businessmen awaited as well textile products,
Food supplies in large numbers, and coconuts!
Very early, Chantal goers transporting those products
Lined up on their way to the city which became noisy
As long as the transporting trucks honked their horn
To announce either their arrival or their departure!
On their part, surveyors and notaries public loved this day too!
Regardless of their name: Jean, Paul, Alexis, or Raymond!
They loved it. For they got money from any transactions declared to them
No matter where the contract took place.

CHAPTER SIX

A Pleasant Trip

Just at the appointed time, the travelers got on board.
They eagerly waited for the bus driver to drop them to the capital City[9].
After they took a seat, they looked at outside.
They looked at their people staying on the homeland
As they exchanged emotional goodbye waves with them!
Who can remain indifferent in seeing a dear friend leave for a very long journey?
"When are you coming back?"
They asked with a sullen air.
"Are you really coming back soon over here?" They asked.

Sometimes, he that witnesses the departure of another from the homeland
Would like to leave the same day too!
That occurs mostly after he realizes that his traveling friend is leaving for real
For a new life to a new place
Where joy, success, and happiness I think are promised!
Thus, many curious ones take their leave from their natal area
As they hanker for treading this Promised Land!
In search for a social ascension!
Or for a success they think can arrive overnight!
However, it takes patience to them!
It takes patience to know about what the future has in store for them abroad!
Or to know whether the beautiful life
That lured them into a foreign place was just an illusion!
So to end this digression,
Let us take a look at the travelers on board this bus.

---

[9]   Port-au-Prince

In that occasion, the autobus *Belle Gitane* welcomed
Notable and humble people living in Chantal neighborhood,
Young and old passengers, married and single people,
Buyers and sellers, teachers and students,
Laymen and religious, civil and military,
People from the urban and from rural areas, lawyers and so on.
All of them were making this journey to the capital city!
And let us say that among all these passengers
With whom Jain and his uncle were making the trip
There were residents or citizens of a foreign country too.
The child and his avuncular guardian could easily recognize the latter
Through the jewelry overloading their neck
Or by their language!

Then the bus left the commercial gathering that swarmed the street.
After few seconds only, it vanished in a dizzying swirl of dust!
Then comic passengers captured universal attention.
They made people laugh in constant explosions
As they told about thousand follies!
Traveler Simil showed how good he was in giving someone the giggles!
He resorted to striking images that tickled people's fancy.
And Jain listened to the wonderful stories
About Bouki[10] marrying the princess
And about his young nephew Malice who as a failing courter
Would like to sadden his uncle by taking his wife!

However, Simil sometimes was out of his mind!
How to trust him when he swore in name of God
That he saw with his own eyes an angel swim close to his house?
Look, Simil said that he saw a water demon
Take care of his hair with a beautiful comb at the so called Montriel[11]
basin!

---

[10]   In the Haitian myths, Malice most of the time outwits his uncle Bouki. Hence
acting like Bouki is behaving like a mindless and gullible person.

[11]   According to the myths, the Montriel Basin would have been called after Mme
Montriel, a resident of Chantal city, who would have been abducted for few days
by the aquatic demon in charge of that river.

He said that this aquatic spirit having seen him
Disappeared by dipping into the waves to join his aquatic world!
Unhappily, there were quite some listeners to accredit that myth
And to see in it a fact that would have happened more than once.
Whether those gullible passengers came from Gauvin or Simite[12],
They came to believe in Simil's fairytale.

Jain however took Simil's joke for a real fiction.
In fact, the young man studied the Bible.
He perfectly knew that today the demons can't appear in bodily form on earth[13];
He recalled that in Noah Time,
After they married pretty women and bred a race of violent giants down here,
The true God, Jehovah, took away from them the power to materialize.
To sum up, the passengers got fun,
Aboard the bus tearing the breeze and going so fast
That it forced the admiration of some and instilled obsession into others.
The entertainment seemed to shorten the day!
For all the travelers wondered at approaching their destination so shortly!
Above all, the jokes had captured their attention
To such a point that they still can think of that trip with great joy!

---

[12]   Gauvin and Simite are located in the vicinity of Chantal.
[13]   Maybe did Jain know what is said in Genesis 6:1-3!

CHAPTER SEVEN

The Castle of Linda Trazileo

Jain and his uncle arrived to the capital City.
On one hand, the boy was happy, optimistic
And so determined to meet his mother!
He hoped that his mom would no longer underestimate his love need.
On the other hand, the uncle was unquiet.
He was conscious that his careless sister would blame him
For surprisingly visiting her with her "undeclared" son!
Upon getting off the bus, they got in a taxi to Turgeau[14].
After fifteen minutes, they already arrived in front of Linda's castle.

That dwelling stood magnificent in the middle of flowerbeds!
It was in that mansion that the mother, now Linda Trazileo,
Had led for seven years a well-charmed existence
Next to her husband, Joshua Trazileo, a masterful accordionist!
Joshua had inherited that property from his defunct father.
He had decided on making it his family's dwelling.
For he preferred that construction than anyone else
Among the multiple houses which he had received in legacy.

The property was surrounded by a high wall of stones
That put its large courtyard out of sight!
To enter it, it was necessary to pass through the barrier only.
Otherwise, one would have to climb on the walls.
In case someone approached the gate at night,
He would certainly hear an unleashed-German shepherd barking inside.
Woe to the strangers!
Thus, Medor, the terrifying dog secured the estate.
On day time, however, they kept the dog on leash
To protect the visitors against the pet that was said to charge people like a lion!

---

[14]   One of the most important towns in Port-au-Prince

Linda Trazileo liked pigeons.
Therefore, she had a large pigeon breeding cage in her backyard!
That's why, sitting in the balcony,
She enjoyed listening their cooing, which caressed all ears,
In the beautiful landscape!
Linda also had an irresistible passion for rearing other birds
Such as turtle dove, peacock, and parrot!
She preferred those birds than hen.
She got the assistance of her maid when taking care of those birds.

No need to say how her dog played an instrumental role
In protecting the poultry at night!
The quadruped patrolled here and there and uttered loud barks.
This way he daunted any potential bird lifters.
Whenever Linda came back from work,
She went straight to the barnyard whence all these oviparous animals
Seeing her flew towards her to get fed.

Linda loved the villa as well for its architecture and its environment.
To tell the truth, she loved roses
More than all the other flowers of her glowing garden!
When she was watching from the terrace,
She could see with admiration
How bees were flying from the laurels to lilies and to daisies!
From splendid Orchids to Scarlet tulips,
From Golden Iris petals to Sunflowers
From the hydrangeas with their bluish charm to charming peonies
And to beautiful miscanthus!
From the cheerful chalet in whitish wallflowers to the bougainvilleas
And to the lovely cactus!

She often paid the service of a gardener to prune the lush leaves
With electric tool or a manual instrument!
Thus, the field offered a beautiful panorama.
And the visitors loved seeing it so beautiful!
They liked to go there! They liked to be there!
To see and admire the wonderful dwelling!

It was in part what charmed the eyes,
When taking a look at the villa of Mme Trazileo,
Not far from the pool where one would be happy admiring this scenery.

In fact, the castle looked like a fortress.
You would be well tempted to take refuge in it in case of natural disaster!
While the castle by its titanic dimension
Captured the attention of every curious passer-by,
It also caused some of them to take a picture of it
And others to go their way with wonderment!

Chapter Eight

A Castle That Raised Different Comments

This castle represented an insignificant part only of Joshua Trazileo's riches.
This "Croesus" possessed for himself twenty castles
That were as enjoyable as that connubial home!
In addition, he also owned restaurants, hotels, and ships.
For that reason, he was considered to be among the wealthiest ones of the city.
Not to say of the country!
If he should take care of his business by himself,
He would have no time to do so.
For that reason he entrusted the management of his properties
To reliable friends who were also his spokesman in some circumstances.

In fact, Mr. Trazileo was born of wealthy parents
Who had bequeathed everything to him as their unique son!
He had been the only one heir of his father,
His father the only one legatee of his grand-parent,
His grand –father the unique son of his rich- great- grand-father.
The latter a grand officer getting always leading position in the country
Got used to enriching himself at the expenses of the public administration!
For of public interest he cared so little!
We can understand that at his death, he left a huge legacy
That would pass from father to son, to grant son, and to great grand-son!
To tell the truth, all they managed their goods wisely.

One day, three passers- by took curiously a look at Linda Trazileo's castle.
As they watched the construction with envy,
They expressed their feelings as follows:

"Oh! How many on earth store up riches!" The first one said.
"They own so much so that they can waste their money!
They can even pay for themselves a round trip in the moon!
Yes! They have enough to no longer work if they want it!

Since long ago, look,
The goods have belonged exclusively to a group of masters
Whose receptacles had been well filled even before their birthday!
Consequently, they die without knowing what shortage and need mean.
For since they came to life in an opulent family,
They found these words already delete from their book!

By contrast, homeless and starving people sleep in the street!
They yearn for their supper in a chronic shortage!
It's what makes them different than the first ones on earth.
Since their birthday, they have missed everything! Absolutely, everything!
As regards joy, they almost ignore this word
Until the day of their extinction!
Alas, while overcome by poverty, they make efforts that prove to be unsuccessful!
They sink into despair and drink their bitter cup!

O God, why do you close your eyes in front of their sufferings?
Why have you blessed the rich and cursed the poor?
Why don't you give the have-not some ease too?
So he can also experience a beautiful day and be sated and happy?
Why have you limited wealth to a small class everywhere?
Why this fence between rich and poor everywhere?
O God! Tell lease!"
Thus spoke the first- unhappy bystander,
As he watched the splendid mansion
And looked at once at a nearby- miserable place
Where many poor people dwelled in a swarm of contiguous cases!

"But is it here only that we can see the difference between wealthy and poor?"
The second asked.
"Ah! Don't the manors inspire viewpoints similar to ours anywhere?
Why don't you realize that this striking contrast between the two classes
Has dated back to a past when classes and casts divided the human kind?
Has God wanted it to be like that?
Has God really wanted some people to get too many goods

As the majority drag on a miserable existence!
Has God really provided the wealthy ones with a rich share?
Has He let most of people struggle along with a tiny part?
Has He overprotected somebody at the expense of others?
Has He placed all the rich on top and all the poor below?
Has He chosen the first ones to be his Apostles
And forgotten the second ones in their worst hassle?
Did God create down here as Aristotle said,
'One social class with the right to command as masters
And another one with the obligation to undergo the yoke as slaves[15]*'*
Is it right, in fact, to imagine that?
Indeed, should we accuse the true God of all this?
Should we accuse Him of empowering someone to enslave someone?
Of reducing in need and keeping as slaves
Those who, having nothing, are looking for a relief?
Of treating them as He pleases in this prison
Where poverty retains its detainees to many respects?"

These were the most controversial issues
Which that mansion raised on behalf of the poor and the wealthy!
Then the third bystander made his intervention:

"Would it be normal, Gentlemen, to consider prosperity
As a proof of heavenly approval
In whatever is done with austerity and pomp on earth?
Gentlemen, leave God out of it all!
In the mind of God, the rich and the poor should be treated the same.
He never judges humans on the basis of their material goods
No matter how opulent or modest their condition was.
Neither our humble condition nor all our prosperity
Can earn us the heavenly favor!
Our fear of Him, this is what He seeks in us!
This is also what is precious in his eyes!
Either poverty or wealth does not qualify anybody
To receive the prize of the eternal life!

---

[15]   See Aristotle's *"Politics" (book I).*

To be safe, both rich and have-not need to behave until the judgment time!

God has always acted fairly
With those owning all the treasures in the World
As much as with those having nothing!
As a matter of fact, He accepts both their sacrifices.

Therefore, if God blessed the wealthy ones only,
How could He send his son Jesus to be born in a modest family?
Did not Joseph occupy a self-effacing -social rung
When God made him the foster father of the announced Messiah?
Did not God know Joseph to be then a humble carpenter?
As for the Virgin Mary who received the favor
To mother Jesus, the main spokesman of God, and the Archangel,
She was honored due to her great piety, not as a rich woman!
Both Joseph and Mary could afford nothing but a pair of birds[16]
So they could present the divine child in the Temple before God!
And that offering was the cheapest one[17], and God accept it
In order to give the human kind his unique son as the greatest gift!

In addition, history has proved that our God
Has been fair also while judging the rich and the poor!
He has been also a fair judge
Who makes his decision without discriminating between the rich and the poor!
In fact, by his right judgments
He brought down monarchs to their graves
Just as He had blessed Lords and Kings!
He had also returned the poor to dust
When the latter spurning him trampled on his laws!

History also has shown that no difference
Has never existed between the humans at the time of misfortune;
For no matter how miserable or opulent they were
They all have been hit together by the same destructive scourges!

[16]   See Luke 2:24.
[17]   See Lev 5:7.

The eruption of Mount Vesuvius has well demonstrated
That any distinction on the basis of the goods is pointless
When a disaster springs!
Which should remind us that
We humans are nothing on earth in the presence of God.
In that day masters and slaves perished all together!
Patricians, plebeians, all of them disappeared!
And today their remains in Pompeii look alike,
So we can remember that all is vanity.
Similarly, in the Middle-Ages,
The plague claimed the life of both lords and villains
As serfs and pages experienced a similar death!

Thus, all our treasures can't save us
Nor can they argue for or against our claim at the Judgment time!
Consequently, let us acquire goods as we keep from sticking to them
Since we know that only God can save us!

Riches are so precarious and fragile
Because we can be wealthy today and become poor tomorrow!
And although prosperity may seem everlasting,
Earthly goods are as ephemeral as our life!
Therefore, we'd better recall that only God deserves glory
And stop making an ostentatious display of our riches!"

This advice ended the conversation among the three bystanders.

CHAPTER NINE

At the Entrance to the Villa

The swift Peugeot dropped them at the sidewalk near the quiet property.
Then Jain and his uncle drew close to the barrier.
From the balcony, the housekeeper saw the taxi and got curious.
She would like to know what visitors dropped by the villa at that time.
Quickly, she got downstairs and headed for the portal to talk to them.
Then she realized soon that they came from far away.

Meanwhile, Jain looked inside through the entrance and uttered a silent soliloquy,
"What a lap of luxury my brothers have lived in!
Unhappy me! Why my mother does not treat me like them?
O God, how come she has turned me down like an unknown child!
O God! Let her make a decision!

Unfortunately, in that evening,
Jain and his uncle could not meet Linda: She was abroad for weeks.
Days ago, she had taken her leave for Europe with her husband, Joshua Trazileo.
Since, she was sailing about touching at some places in Italy,
Including Capua, Sicily, Naples, and Rome!

Upon knowing about that, Jain was so disappointed
That he felt close to tears!
However, in front of the maid, he feigned to be calm
Like a bewildered warrior who summons up his courage!
He had expected to see his mother and then to go back gladly home!
He had been so eager to slip into her lap!
And to enjoy her maternal love which he never knew as a neglected child!
But since Linda was out of state,
Jain and his uncle were welcomed to the dwelling of someone else living nearby.
The latter had been a friend to the deceased grand-mother.

That's why he volunteered to assist the boy until Linda comes back from her trip.

Therefore, Jain stayed there and longed after seeing his mom.

He was looking forward to seeing her and to admiring her some more!

He was eager to hear his mother calling him her son at least!

He got a craving to fill the gap between him and her,

A gap that has kept them separated since he was born!

In fact, his biggest concern was this emotional void!

This constant feeling of frustration that took root in his non- mothered- childhood!

Then he was mad at Linda who had likely denied him as her son.

And he felt crushed for that.

He would have liked the defunct-grand mother

To never tell him about Linda coming back!

For that news had instilled in him so much delight

As does a tasty small piece of food in a hungry palate!

However, although Linda had come home, she did not appease him.

For now being a guest in Bel-Air[18], he was still waiting for this mother

And thrived to endure his pain as Job his boil!

Nevertheless, he hoped his situation would change one day.

In the meantime, Linda and her husband Joshua were having fun in Italy.

They were enjoying themselves on pleasure trip!

They were leading a profligate life!

And they were affording the most expensive hotels, meals, and parties.

---

[18]   One of the sixteen hills in Port-au-Prince, Haiti.

CHAPTER TEN

The Ancestors of Joshua Trazileo

Joshua Trazileo was making his twentieth trip to Italy
Through which he planned to walk his wife within a month.
Why did he travel to Italy and not to France?
We should ask that question with considering that
Since his childhood he liked talking about the Eternal City[19].

But upon pondering over his obsession for that country,
We will realize that he had inherited his Italophilia from his maternal grandma.
In fact, not only had been Joshua's maternal ancestor an Italian- woman born,
She had also died and had been buried in her Italian motherland too.

After she was born in Venice, Joshua's grandmother was called Denise,
Following the choice of her father, a Frenchman from Nantes;
No one knows about the reason why her father was so crazy about that name.
Denise's father was a gondolier,
Therefore, we can admit that Denise grew up in a humble family.
As a sea worker, her dad, however, liked his occupation
For the real fun which it provided to him!
Indeed, every day, he had to paddle up his boat on a Venetian channel
With travelers coming from all over the World!
And he enjoyed cheering them up during ineffable tours.

O God, what heart could remain emotionless
When this seaman propelled his gondola with some visitors on board
And at once enchanted all ears through his romantic barcarolles?
What sea lover could experience more pleasure
When seated on board his flat-bottomed boat, he watched the aquatic avenue

---

[19]   So is called Rome.

That mirrored all under the shining sun?

However, although Denise's father did not make too much money,
He made her a high-skilled woman.
In France, she studied business and Law.
She got used to travelling too, which led her to a thousand places.
Nevertheless, she preferred journeying on board a ship than on aircraft.
For, since she was so good at swimming!
She thought she could survive a shipwreck better than a plane crash.
And she fully remembered her euphoric moments during exciting cruises
By which she had been across all the continents;
For so early! She had a burning desire for exploring the whole- entire
World!

Once ago, during a cruise alongside Mexico,
Denise met Claude Trazileo, the future grandfather to Joshua Trazileo.
Then she discovered in Claude a so smart young man!
Right away she fell ablaze with passion for him!

In that day, Claude had just landed in the same Mexican site as she,
Yet had he been on board a different boat.
This unexpected encounter occurred in Oaxaca, near Acapulco,
In a mural Museum where was exposed the artistic work of Diego Riviera.

It was there precisely that Denise fell in love with Claude
And then also began their love history
When both of them came to know
How they had a common passion for the Aztec history.
To tell the truth, Denise was few knowledgeable in that topic.

In this occasion Claude and Denise were watching together
A fresco showing Conquistador Cortes with his hand tainted with blood.
In reality, that artistic work had been made up by Riviera[20]
In order to tell about the killings and tortures

---

[20] Diego Rivera (1886-1957) a Mexican muralist painter. Most of most of his frescoes reproduce historical and social facts.

That Cortes[21] had inflicted to the Indians.
Since Claude saw Denise getting lost in this fresco as he,
He took advantage to break the ice and then made her acquaintance.
As for her, she seized the opportunity to engage a dialogue with him
About the civilizations which left their multi-centennial traces on that land
Through monuments that have been saved at all costs.

The two interlocutors plunged their gaze far away into the past,
Into a past which on the Alban Mount[22]
Still gives a great testimony today about the Toltecs[23]' lifestyle
As much as about the Zapotecs who had lived there long ago!
Finally, they came to talk of Christopher Columbus having discovered Haiti.
Once more, Denise took the opportunity
To recollect so many things from which she had heard.
For she found in Claude a so fecund mind!

"Could you remind me of the hardship through which
The early inhabitants of Haiti went,
I mean the adversities which these aborigines experienced
After the Columbus' caravels dropped their anchors into the sea of this rich land?"

Claude began speaking of the historical facts and of the dark episodes
In which the Caciques Anacaona, Caonabo[24], and Henry[25] took place.
He refreshed her memory on these events which already inspired so many odes!

"At that time, he said, Columbus and his companions

---

[21] Herman Cortes, Spanish conqueror, took over the Mexico in 1519 and ended the Aztec empire in 1521.

[22] Mount Alban is located in the Southern Mexican State of Oaxaca.

[23] The Toltecs and the Zapotecs, two Indian communities having lived in Mexico before the Aztecs.

[24] Caonabo and Anacaona two of the five caciques or kings of Haiti to the arrival of the Spaniards led by Christopher Columbus.

[25] Last Cacique of Haiti under the Spanish colonization.

Had just landed in Haiti.

They saw gold everywhere! So much gold so that

They thought that they were treading the terrestrial paradise!

All over the place on their steps, the so precious metal was shining!

And they had trouble believing it!

They thought that they were wrapped in dream in daylight!

Gold on the ways! Gold on the beaches! That was incredible!

And everything at which they gazed also enchanted them:

Beautiful water lilies, green groves noisy of avian cries!

Green hill slopes which the blue waves caressed!

Waters in which impetuous carps voluptuously jumped

And attracted fishermen under the breeze!

Look, they thought that they had come to tread a new land

Where no one had seen any misfortunes crack down!

Because all was only joy, exultation, and happiness

Absolute tranquility and eternal peace

For the native who loved frequent naps and a deep sleep under fruit trees

And who then had to worry about nothing!

Nor about a better day and a disastrous future:

Agriculture and fishing sated their alimentary needs!

As they only had to braid palm of *Latania,* or to weave cotton and get dressed!

And they led happy their frugal existence!

In absolute peace as an independent people!

And God donated them everything!

As soon as Columbus and his companions saw these islanders,

They quickly called them Indians for their copper color,

For they looked like the people of India,

In which they thought that they had landed!

Haiti, corner of land bristling with mountains

And fascinating through its beautiful nature,

Of all these pilgrims ignited the desire and the envy

And caused at once to arouse in their mind a dream

Which the natives could never discover:

Resorting to trickery and betrayal to liquidate the leaders of this island,
Who, however, had welcomed them with the greatest cordiality!
And that way the heartless conquistadors managed to harness the naive nation!
Then, barbarity started ruling under wealth-thirsty executioners' hands,
Who perpetrated tortures, hanging, and killings against them!
And also sent them to death at hunting-dogs' jaws!
Or under shooting from musketeers!

Since then, no more muse, no more songs by them!
Their poets or *sambas* fell into the greatest "silence!"
And their poetry died as well across so many misdeeds!
Their pitiless conquerors deemed it to be normal
To victimize them by means of any life destroying actions!
Therefore, Sun stopped shining for those "Indians"!
Yet, was in the name of love and of peace
That these explorers discovered America!
Yet, did Columbus wear a Bible the same day that he landed in Quisqueya!
Alas! His companions ignored the content of this sacred Book
From which no one had heard on this land before they came!
They had, however, well known the Divine word in the language of Cervantes! And despite all, they did what they did against those innocent victims!
What crime had they committed? Those natives to perish that way!
Shame on whoever had tainted his hand with their pitiable blood!
Shame on whoever got enriched with their gold!
May the judgment of the heaven claim the blood of these innocent!"
Thus, had spoken Claude to the Venetian woman who liked history so much!
She took pity on those inhabitants who had died for their golden mines.

CHAPTER ELEVEN

They Spoke of Poetry too!

Denise having heard that narration was moved to tears.
Hence, Claude guided the conversation to another topic.
He moved forward to the poetic ground
Which he thought includes much more charm to brighten Denise up.
And he was right!
For beyond the fact that Denise cordially appreciated beautiful verses,
She practiced poetry too
And delighted so much in reading her own lines!

"Madam, would you mind discussing a literary issue with me? » Claude asked.
"Not at all," Denise replied.
"Whether a poet belongs to our era or had existed long ago," Claude said,
"What real interest there is in studying his verses?
Would it be just for our entertainment only
That they teach us about a poet like Baudelaire or like Lafontaine?"

"Many have answered these beautiful questions in different ways." Denise said.
"As for me, I have found in poetry a good friend.
For like music, it cheers me up.
Really, through a poem I may find a good message to remind me
That we all have similar feelings and go through hardships
Across which we were supposed to become wise!

In fact, who has sung the bitterness of love?
Whom our disappointments sadden at first?
Who has particularly felt bad when a disaster ravages a beautiful landscape?
Whom this beautiful universe, the work of the one true God,
Puts into ecstasy when he wakes up
And that the firmament spreads its wonders in front of him
And tells him, 'be happy, my child'?

This state of mind belongs to the poet, who regardless of his literary preference,
Strives to create a work for all,
For all those who someday will recognize themselves throughout his own pages!
For example, there is nothing unreal in the love which von Goethe[26],
The Frankfurt poet, celebrated when telling his sweetheart
What transport brings him by many nights to her angelic face!
Nor is there something esoteric
In the ineffable love which Shakespeare depicts!
We will meet I think a Juliet and a Romeo everywhere
As long as people are burning of an erotic flame!
Choose whomever you want
Among the literary names which instill in readers sorrow, or happiness!
Pick up the vengeful Hermione and the weeping Andromaque[27],
You'll realize that each one has character traits which are similar to ours.

The ardent passion igniting the poets in any languages
Has its equivalent in all societies
Where any love poet I think will feel appropriate
To celebrate his romantic conquests and grieve his defeat!
Hence, I feel relieved to know that through the space and the time,
A poet is someone who seeks a confidant for his sorrow.
And this is what I think Ovid in his Roman century did in his love poem
Where he portrays his attractive wife Corinne as an unfaithful woman,
A jealous, a fickle, and a greedy wife!
When a bard talks so about his own problems
Or tells us how great his suffering was,
He will find certainly other writers to make the same confession as he.
Because over time it is the same experience
Bringing hearts to break their silence by raising their voices of singers of love!

---

[26]   "*Welcome and Farewell*", a poem in which Goethe describes his night-equestrian trips to his sweetheart.

[27]   Hermione and Andromaque, two characters in "*Andromaque*", a tragedy by Jean Racine.

Therefore, who does not know about the betrayed poets?
Or those who have sung in many gloomy verses
A love devoid of sunlight and roses, a hopeless and a misunderstood one!

However, if I single the grief of the poets out,
It does not follow that I ignore their elation!
Since their existence includes charms as well
And that their desperation sometimes gives way to celebration!
Thus, with reading verses I have realized that we are nearly the same everywhere!
And that poetry offers the jovial one and the sad one as well the same opportunities
To let speak their mind for the sake of whoever wants to hear them!

However, I think that poetry goes beyond the tears and the laughter
Of an emotional-human being.
I think that a good poetry should also come out of the writer's heart
And scan his society of which facts and realities it should reflect,
No matter what the features of that social body are:
Piety, paganism, virtue, crime and so on!
And this is what distinguishes one poet from another:
The social context to which he belongs,
And also the creed of the group he follows,
While his feeling remains the same as ours!"

"Absolutely, Madam, I share your opinion". Claude continued.
I agree with the viewpoint that poetry should mirror people's social environment.
To back up this opinion,
We just need to see how Horace, the Latin poet, talked of his Roman city.
In his Odes, he shows ancient- Roman ladies leading a lustful life;
He describes a Roman smiling and lively nature.
He sings out the falling night and the rising day in Rome!
He says how from dawn to dusk, the dwellers of the Roman city, full of urbanity
Go their ways admiring beautiful gardens and green groves!

In the Horace's verses, the Roman citizens are proud of their heroic feats,
And of the wars having blown out anywhere in the imperial territory,
Wars which they always won from spring to winter,
Both the Gallic conflicts and the Punic wars!

Horace shows a Roman city moving with people going back and forth
And craving for erotic love and feminine grace!
He presents the Epicureans enchanted by attractive and elegant women
Who appealed to the wealthy ones seeking enjoyment at any price!
He says what happened nightly at the doorway of a promiscuous woman
And shows the anxious womanizers lining up in front of her house
Where they would stay very late far away from their families!

"However, not only did the Roman poetry reflect the urban areas,
It also sends back the lifestyle of the countryside writers,
Who found a source of inspiration in the peace of their rustic environment!
In fact, civil unrest as much as fighting reigning in the Roman city
Conflicted with pastoral poetry!
Thus, it was well near their herds in a rustic-quiet place
That bucolic poet enjoyed themselves.
Really, too much noise in the Roman City!
Too much noise when the Roman army in triumph was there!
And that in the neck of the war captive was sinking a cutlass!
Too many horrors in these places during the civil wars!
Too much bloodshed in Rome when Caesar prevailed on his rival Pompey[28]
Of whom defeated hordes should flee before it was too late!
Too much blood in the Roman city

---

[28]   In the year 60 BC, the first Roman triumvirate consisted of Julius Caesar, of
Gnaeus Pompey, and Crassus Lucinius. Incidentally, to consolidate that political
alliance, Pompey married Julia, the daughter of Julius Caesar, which, however,
did not preclude the stepfather and his son in law from indulging in a political
rivalry between each other. Caesar was appointed governor of Cisalpine Gaul,
Pompey of Spain, and Crassus of Syria. Crassus was killed in the war against the
Parthian in AD 53, which would facilitate the civil war between the two rivals,
Caesar and Pompey, in the year 50. Caesar defeated his son-in-law as evidenced
by historians.

While even Cicero[29] running away from his executioners evacuated it
And that despite his escape, he was caught and killed
For fighting the merciless triumvirs[30]!
Too much civil unrest in struggling for power!

And Propertius and Tibullus liked the countryside
Where following the harvest they piled up the straws
And burned them to further sow with hope!
And this frugal life among the sheep which they secured with their hunting dogs,
As poets, they liked it in their rural class!
Where they got everything: water, bread, and wine!
And playing their flute in the mist of their fields,
They missed nothing, close to Cynthia, and near Delia
Into the laps of their beautiful wives, they enjoyed their life
That was sated with their women's love all the time!"

"O my friend, so many things to say on the poets and on their feelings!"
Denise said.
"We need much more time to speak! Today, I was so delighted to meet you!
But now, alas, I should take my leave!
Here is my card, and feel free to contact me!
I already anticipate my pining after hearing from you!"

---

[29]   The full name of this Roman orator was Marcus Tullius Cicero. Politician, philosopher, lawyer and orator, he left a work could not be more immense. He was author of works such *"For Catiline"*, *" For Archias"*, *"For Milo"*, *"For Sulla"*, *"Philippics"*, *"Against Caecilius"*, *"Dialogues"*, *"Paradoxes"* and so on.

[30]   These were the members of the second Roman triumvirate that was composed of Octavian, Marc Antony, and Lepidus. As the killers amputated Cicero's hands, they blamed him for writing against Marc Antony.

CHAPTER TWELVE

To the Next Level

Claude left Denise with a so good impression on him!

That's why coming back to the ship she thought that he was a living encyclopedia,

A melting pot of cultures, and a prodigious mind!

After returning to her homeland, she felt enamored of him so profoundly that

She promptly invited him to Venice!

Claude on his side accepted her invitation!

A week later, he traveled to Italy and made acquaintance with her parent.

And the latter cordially welcomed him.

As experienced parents they saw in that visit the prelude of something deeper

Due to the great interest their daughter showed in Claude!

And guess what! They were right.

Claude and Denise fell in love with each other.

Their true love overrode all impediments to their relationship.

Everything was working so perfectly between them

That Denise and her parent made a trip to Claude's country few months later.

These Venetian, visiting Port-au-Prince for the first time, loved Turgeau.

They realized that the temperature of that country

Was almost similar to Lyon's where they had spent their last vacation!

In fact, there are not enough words in the dictionary to describe the hospitality

Which all the Trazileo showed to their future Venetian allied!

They had never welcomed anybody that much in their whole- entire history!

Shortly, it is to say that Denise's parents were treated like royals!

By the time, Claude and Denise got engaged and expected to get married soon!

O God! They experienced the same attachment as Paul and Virginie[31]!

Nothing could fail their love! Not even the unexpected trials of life.

The following fact is going to show it.

---

[31]   Two young characters of *"Paul et Virginie"*, a novel by Jacques-Henry Bernadin de Saint- Pierre.

CHAPTER THIRTEEN

A Jealous Fiancée

As an engaged woman, Denise was very jealous,
Which Claude, however, failed to realize!
One day that she and Claude were invited to a party in Venice,
Claude naively took the liberty of dancing with a beautiful lady from Andalusia.
Upon seeing that, Denise grew indignant and threw herself at his dance partner
Slapped her on the face, and untied her hairstyles.
Fortunately, people intervened right away to fix the problem.
After that incident, Claude felt so disappointed
That early in the next day
He folded his luggage and went back to his country
Without telling anybody where he went!
Immediately, Denise realized that she had made a huge mistake.
She wasted her time searching for him everywhere to apologize.
However, her fiancé went into hiding.
Then she understood that a nice letter might calm him down
And stop him from cancelling himself.
Therefore, she made this apology in hope to restore their relationship.

"You who cruelly gleam through your absence,
Have you sounded the death knell for my sweet existence?
I already traveled the world seeking you!
Of dens and forests I taunted the danger!
In the bottom of the oceans I haven't seen you!
And to the abyssal shadow, I believed you went down!
Have you moved to another planet?
For the present, Honey, are you become the captive of another queen
To be retained in her backyard forever?
Are you caught in the nets of an invincible love so much so that
You forget about me?
It is for real you have dropped me!

Me to whom you promised the most splendid palaces in the World!
For now, where are the charming words
By which you conquered my invincible heart?
Where is the irresistible prayer that gave you what no one else except you
Could receive from me?
I mean my virginal face glowing with the charm of a rose
Whose fragrance brightens the gloomiest hearts!
My singular charm which stood hundred suitors in ecstasy before me
And took their timidity to its peak
So that passing trembling and disturbed before my face,
They vainly implored my inexorable flame!

Is that your manner to thank me, Honey?
By cancelling yourself for a month?
If you eternally turn your back to me,
Do it without inflicting me this deadly silence!
Therefore, allow my downcast soul to plead for myself
Before you kill me!
Before I see my head falling by your own hands!

Pity on me! On my knees I confess to my fault to you!
Then! You will know if of all the crimes, slapping a rival is the worst one!
And if there still is some pity in your heart, Baby,
Thrive to untie the string of a condemned one."

Thus had spoken Denise at the peak of her affliction!
She wanted to turn that page so quickly!
She was concerned about Claude's passion being gone due to her mistake!
She wondered whether the incident would have caused him to break-up
for real!

Through this test now she knew that she really loved him
For she remained sad since he had disappeared!
Plunged into the depths of despair, she vainly tried to get off her distress.
Then she knew well how the bite of love opposes our joy and our happiness!
And how the happiness which love gives
Can sometime have only the lifespan of a flower!

She also realized that
We can't experience an infinite happiness by ill-treating our best friend!
And that in case we hurt our intimate one,
We must settle the case before night comes!

Claude receiving that letter changed his mind.
For he too was affected by the separation which
He thought was the appropriate decision in that circumstance.
In fact, all the Trazileo would react the same way!
They shy away from any women whom anger can move to act so violently!
And all of them facing such a difficulty would have the same feeling!
I know them!
Claude appreciated that his fiancée begged his pardon
And that she sought an epistolary way to finally get him back.
He thought he should get back quickly to her to comfort her.
Actually, he was pining over her beautiful face
And he would like to fly immediately toward her if he could!

In fact, Claude surrendering intended to reassure promptly Denise.
He knew that a regretful fiancée can change her mind
If undergoing an excessive disdain on the part of her future husband.
As a reader of Honoré de Balzac
He would dislike repeating the same mistake as Montriveau.
That high-ranked officer in the military [32]
Gets mad at the duchess, his aristocratic girlfriend,
Who influenced by the strict principles of her noble class,
Had constantly kept him as distantly as possible in their relationship;
To take revenge, the unhappy boyfriend dissimulating his wrath
Has her abducted by his soldiers!
For now, the highborn-humiliated girlfriend remembering
That her prejudice was out of limit

---

[32]   In *"The Duchess of Langeais"*, novel by Honoré de Balzac, Mr. Montriveau getting revenge on his girlfriend, who had hurt him with her puritanical manners, makes the mistake of inflicting an excessive humiliation on her. His aristocratic sweetheart, having lost all hope of reconciliation with him, would have already found in the Carmelite convent the balm of her grief in the very moment when her lover tries in vain to get her out of her cloister after seeking her for long.

Vainly tries to appease her resentful boy friend and to prove him her love!
We know how this fairytale ends!
This vengeful fiancé failed to know how long he should keep silent
At his remorseful sweetheart!
Alas! When he wants to get back to her, she will be already a nun.

Fortunately, Claude knowing about that novel got back to Denise quickly!
Here is how he reacted to her letter.

"Whatever the misdeed which your heart blames on you
To such an extent that you miss your very joy,
If you really feel wrong in your inner conscience,
Stop thinking that you disqualify from pardon.

For happy you if you really realize
That you have hugely offended your neighbor
And that your fault has filled your whole soul with remorse!
You should be forgiven since you're really sorry!

Therefore you must avoid making the same mistake
For fear that you might come to harden your conscience!
And you will need to make a tremendous effort
To stay absolutely away from the pathway which
Alas, you had followed to your great suffering!"

Since then, the two fiancés remained stuck to each other.
Their engagement created a remarkable symbiosis between their two families.
Finally, they united their lives by the matrimonial-sacred bond...
After that, they lived in Montagne Noire.
To tell the truth, Denise loved that place!
It is there that she gave birth to Robert Trazileo their unique son.
As for Robert Trazileo,
He grew up and married Nathalie the daughter of a Syrian merchant
Who owned a bus Company in Turgeau.
When Robert was twenty-five years old,
He became the father of Joshua Trazileo.

Joshua Trazileo was spoiled by his grandmother Denise.

In summer time, his grandma got accustomed to going abroad with him.
However, when Joshua married Linda, the mother of Jain,
Denise was already dead and buried in Italy.
His father Robert Trazileo already died in his way to Saint-Marc, Haiti.
Claude, Trazileo his grand-father had expired of a heart attack the same year.
Then Joshua was almost alone.

After so many cases of mortality in the Trazileo family,
Nathalie wanted to cheer her unique son Joshua up.
That's why she tried to marry him with the gorgeous Julie.
Unhappily, things went wrong for Joshua and Julie.
Then Joshua striving to forget about his deception married Linda
Whom he loved to distraction!
Linda, Jain's mother, will make him forget about all his hard times.
Five years later, Nathalie, Joshua mother, died.
At that moment Joshua wanted to die too,
However, his wife Linda consoled him so soon!

CHAPTER FOURTEEN

Jain Waiting for his Mother

Jain looked forward to seeing his mother coming back from vacation.
By the time, he would go to a Mariani[33] beach, not too far from his host's town.
By an afternoon, the young man got to the seashore with his uncle.
He got ready to experience a pelagic enjoyment in that day.
It was Saturday, as usually the water was so exciting!
Sea lovers organized nautical games;
They floated on their back; they swam and they did aquatic ski.
They also engaged in competition on board canoes.
All that was so amazing for the apprentice swimmers!
People got drunk with alcohol or with any cocktails
Which they took as aphrodisiac!
And while skilled dancers dandled with a fluttering rhythm,
Everyone delighted in the musical compositions executed by troubadours!
No need to say how such things appealed to the visitors!

"How happy I am to be here!" Then Jain exclaimed after he discovered that world.
Now using his binocular,
He made his focal point of anything he could observe from afar:
Trading ships which were pulled to the harbor,
Canoes propelled by exhausted paddlers,
And the eternal seamen whom the fisheries work kept busy.

Jain took a sympathetic look at the fishermen
Who stayed alone from afar on the sea, especially when the weather is clement!
His fun, however, is short lasting!
All of a sudden, he sinks himself into deep despair!
Thinking that his mom would never come back

---

[33] In the south of Port-au-Prince.

And that he could no longer see her again someday!

Dream all that!

For Jain knew nothing concerning the reasons for Linda's long journey!

Knowing about it would appease him a lot!

It would keep him from making unwise conclusions!

Anyways, his swimming relieved him from his distress a little!

Back home, he continued to focus on his mom.

And he wondered whether or not he was vainly waiting for her.

CHAPTER FIFTEEN

The Reasons behind Linda's Trip

In the meantime, Linda Trazileo knew nothing about the grief of her son.
And nestled in the arms of her affectionate husband,
She was experiencing an unparalleled happiness.
Oh! How long she had been waiting for that trip!
What condition could better match her ecstasy when seeing her dream come true?
Could it be this of the Eden garden?
Could her euphoria be compared to a blissful Nirvana?
To tell the truth, it was not by accident
That Linda had yearned for traveling to Europe.
She had always heard her husband exalting all his fantastic journeys
With his defunct Grandma Denise!
She had learned so many wonderful things from Joshua's visits to Italy
That she became more and more obsessed with the envy to tour the World too!

In reality, both Joshua and Denise used to spend happy vacations over there.
As a learned woman, the grand-mother liked traveling
To appreciate different artworks anywhere she went.
And since Joshua was her unique- spoiled grandson,
She always seized the opportunity to travel with him to develop his intelligence.
And Joshua as a smart boy took advantage to ingratiate himself with her.
He always showed her gratitude and love in turn
For any historical sites which she visited with him.

No need to say how such journeys were profitable to the young man
Becoming a High School student!
Once upon a time, his Latin teacher talking about the Second Punic war,
Gave a class assignment about
"Hannibal frightening the besieging Romans from the peak of the Alps,"

In that occasion, Joshua felt proud to talk about his previous visit to that place
Where that historical event occurred centuries ago!

For now, we can understand why Joshua getting married
Delighted in showing to his attractive wife
Anything by which his defunct grandmother enlivened his soul!

Effectively, Joshua showed his spouse all what she had learned only in the books!
I mean, he showed her things that are evocative of the Ancient Latin leaders
Such as the monuments which remain an eloquent testimony of a glorious past!
Though with her beloved husband, Linda trod the land of a line of Roman kings
From Romulus to Tarquinius the Superbus
And tried to recollect all facts inflaming her passion for the Roman history!

Moreover, Joshua found in that journey with Linda
A way to forget about Julie, his ex fiancée,
Who deceiving him, left him so desperate and tearful!
For when Linda came to Joshua's life,
Julie splitting up with him had just darkened his existence.
At that time, Linda who had learned from her bad experience...
Tried to be as attractive as possible so that one could compare her to an artwork,
To an artwork created under inspiration by a gifted artist!
She was so gorgeous that one could be tempted
To call her Mona Lisa's daughter!
And, I cannot swear, even Leonardo da Vinci should have been be very careful
If he had to realize her portrait and remain as famous as he is today!

Linda's virginal face would mislead any falling angel
Who would hardly believe that she was already a mother!
Moreover her civility, her tenderness, and her good mood
Gained her respect and appreciation from everyone!

Accordingly, she was the treasure about which Joshua dreamed
As an orphan in search for moral support and consolation!
Hence one day, here he is, imploring successfully her love!

Shortly, Linda and Joshua got engaged.
And since then enchanting Joshua with her beautiful appearance,
She backed out all his cruel thoughts from his mind!
Now engaged to Linda,
Joshua stopped shedding tears on that unexpected separation!
What an endless lament
He used to utter while longing for that defunct relationship!
Here is how he grieved his misfortune:

"She was there like a queen in the throne of my heart
As she expertly feigned to yearn for our marriage!
As constantly I dreamed of that oncoming day!
Look how she was the unique object of my great love
And how she seemed to appreciate my dedication to herself!
Before she said a word, I was there for her!
Her wishes I executed as an order!
Her feet I protected against all stumbling stones!
So no difficulty could embitter her life!
And I did whatever could then make her happy
While I really felt blessed in her tender arms!

Really, she was I thought the apple of my eyes!
And I prioritized her choices over my own!
I even gave her right on all my belongings!
For not only I saw in her my unique hope
I perfectly trusted her and so blindly I loved her!

And why not, since next to her I felt worriless?
Why not, since in her presence I found my happiness
And the inexhaustible source of my welfare!
Why not, when I thought that she was the sole on earth
To gain both my loyalty and my attachment!

Oh! I thirsted for that day to see me take the oat
To love her forever and give myself to her!
I hankered for that day to see our singleness
Go out of our life in the presence of God and before all!
For all the steps I made to concretize that dream
Which all sincere- engaged women are waiting for!

I had already prepared our conjugal dwelling, which seemed to fill her heart
With an unrivaled joy!
I had anticipated seeing our children born in that blissful haven of peace!
However, sometimes, disaster comes to knock on your door,
And whereas it makes us its chosen-cursed focus,
It puts our existence alas upside down!
And then mercilessly leaves you in hopelessness:
My ungrateful Julie abandoned me, I mean.
Getting married with me was not her real purpose!
She only wanted me to be her provider!
It was too late for me to realize that despite my efforts to make her happy
She never ever loved me!"

Thus, Joshua grieved every day all his suffering
Until the day Linda came to his existence
And stopped his uttering such a moan of despair!
His journey to Italy also will cheer him up
And erase that sad remembrance from his mind.

CHAPTER SIXTEEN

Welcome to Venice!

Of all the Italy then was Venice the favorite land of Joshua.

This is well explained by the fact that Denise, his grandma, had been a Venetian.

Then we can understand that Joshua felt home whenever coming to that country!

Whether he traveled alone, or escorted by a co-journeyer,

The fact remained that he was welcome to the Venice's shores.

Actually, with his wife he came to that country.

He was still welcome by his Venetian friends and relatives.

Then one of them, Alberto, offered hospitality to the visiting couple.

Joshua, however, felt obliged to decline that invitation.

For months earlier he had made a reservation at a nearby island!

Nevertheless, he accepted Alberto's invitation to a get-together.

Linda greatly appreciated the cordiality with which they received them.

In fact, she loved the kind of person like Alberto,

Who on his hand was looking forward to receiving them so warmly!

Sincerely, he had a particular reason to treat them with that conviviality:

This old Venetian, in fact, remembered his wonderful vacations in Haiti,

Where he had always been treated like a prince!

He still kept an admirable album of photographs

Which he had taken, not too long ago, from different locations in that country!

He still could talk of his trips to Port-Salut, to Corail, to Camp-Perrin, and so on!

He loved those places and could say with sincere words how beautiful they were.

As for the city of Jacmel of which mountains and sea amazed him,

He would spend an entire day talking about it.

He spoke of these areas as if he had just visited them one day ago only!

Don't mention Labadie. He was so crazy for that place

In which he saw as sings a local poet a little paradise!

Really, although Alberto was an outsider,
He knew the country more than Joshua Trazileo. What a paradox!
Sometimes, the visitor may know your country better than you
To such a point that he knows better than you the town where you were born!
Worse yet, can the visitor be more knowledgeable than you in your own history
So extensively that at anytime you may wonder at his exposé on your past!
The fact remains that sometimes we tour the World
And we forget about our own land.

CHAPTER SEVENTEEN

In the Murano Island

By this afternoon, the Murano Island got busy as usually.
Under the heat of August, the water gave off its lagoon smell with all its strength.
The sun was still igniting!
From near and from afar, the sunlight was reflected both by the blue waves
And by the splendid glassworks, which forced everyone admiration!
The gondoliers crisscrossed the sea and took everywhere their passengers
Who wondered at the aquatic show!
"Look! A city on the water! It's not like home!"
Some visitors said on a euphoric tone.

If the eyes were satisfied with the spectacle of the day,
The ears as well relished, o God, the serenades on board the gondolas
And during all the tours, which made all sick of Venice!
Venice knows how to charm her lovers coming from everywhere!
All those who are seduced by the softness of her romantic voice!
Then, hearing that voice, we can forget about everything!
And when we remember it, we long for it!

In that afternoon, on board a *vaporeto*,
Joshua and his wife arrived to that island where the beautiful- old couple Alberto,
With calm and joviality waited for their arrival for the dinner.
"Welcome to my humble dwelling!" Then the old man said.
"Make yourself at home, please!
We have cooked for you a meal, we hope, will appeal to you, beloved children!"

And Linda once again felt happy to be so warmheartedly welcomed to the family!
She appreciated the fact that Andrea Alberto had been yearning for knowing her

And seeing how attractive she was.

Married with Alberto, Andrea, an Italian woman was from Venice as well.
As a masterful pianist, she was deemed to be an excellent musician.
And she sang very well too!

Alberto introduced the invited couple to Jaquelin,
His thirty-years-old guest coming from Paris.
Jaquelin was a lawyer; he was imbued with literary knowledge too.
He planned to spend three days with Alberto.
He felt well pleased to find himself there as usually when he came to that place.

Alberto introduced Adele, Jaquelin's wife, a French woman.
As a French woman born in La Rochelle, she was a gynecologist.
She loved both sea and pleasures trip.
Adele was the adopted daughter of the couple Alberto.
While living in France, she often came with her husband to her adoptive parents.
And the old couple felt proud of Adele
Whom they had adopted when she turned eight!

We must not forget about Madam Mangelli
Whose services the old couple had paid so expensively!
Physically, that cordon blue was as thin as the letter I.
In fact, there were seven people to enjoy that dinner,
All of them with their cheerful mind, entertained by the festive atmosphere
Which several elements were making more and more delightful.
The table was almost ready, and to whet everybody's appetite,
Ms. Mangelli came with a lovely smile and served some wine, and some Martini.

On the table then dressed in white tablecloth,
Set in French style were the cutleries, which constantly twinkled and yearned for
The consumption of so multiple foods;

This tablecloth was embroidered with exotic drawings of a tropical landscape:
Coconut trees, cattle, small paths, and ploughmen at work,
A true depiction of the pastoral life!

As regards the menu, we must admit that
Alberto wanted in his own way honor Joshua and Linda
To whom he demonstrated a particular affection in this circumstance:
A triple- cultural menu he offered, which should taste good to every palate!
Haitian, Italian, and French meal and desserts he had ordered from Ms. Mangelli.

Andrea announced that the table was ready.
At the round table a man with a woman she had alternated by small cartons.
In that occasion, I don't know why
She separated each husband from his wife at the table.
Therefore Joshua Trazileo, the guest of honor,
Could see through the front door everything happening outside
As he heard the engine of these *vaporetti* on the busy water!

A short prayer Alberto pronounced thanking God for allowing his guests
To join him and Andrea and eat this meal with them!
Ah! How brief he was definitely!
During the reception, a tender concerto by Mozart fondled the guests' ears
While in the room lit like by daylight
All noses got wondered at the smell of the meal!

In the meantime, all people kept silent. Who would break the ice?
Alberto started telling about a short- funny tale.
Since then, the liveliness of the ambiance was resumed.
For each guest found something to talk about:

Jaquelin said that the human laws are unfair but that without them
Our society would grapple with too many troubles and with too much injustice.

That viewpoint reminds Joshua of another issue about which he really cared:
The loneliness of fatherless children, which is a hardship for the single mothers!

As for Adele, she spoke of teen mothers in childbirth on a daily basis,
Disappointing cases which she thought happened less frequently years ago
When the youth got less involved too early in a love affair!

To sum up, they jumped from rooster to donkey.
Then Alberto felt sorry for the defunct Denise missing that moment!

Linda exposed about her great surprise.
According to her report, one day before, she had been amazed
When her cicerone told her about the poet Musset having lost his wife in Venice!
She said how astonished she had been to know that a primary care doctor
Took the romantic poet's wife in that country,
A thing about which everyone knew in Venice centuries ago!
Linda said that at her teenage
She had learned about the poet breaking up with his wife,
A cruel deception over which Musset bewailed in *Les Nuits!*[34]
But that now only she knew where the incident occurred!
At this time, everybody around the table wanted to know more deeply
Why the poet got betrayed by Sand[35] in Venice
Where they came a winter and exposed their love to the worst defeat!
And since all the guests loved the romantic poetry
Of which Musset was a great representative,
They wanted to know more about that bard who went through that trial long ago.

---

[34] Between 1835 and 1837 Alfred de Musset orchestrated his suffering in poems such as *"The Night of May"*, *"The Night of December"*, *"The Night of August"* and *"The Night of October"*.

[35] George Sand (1804-1876) was the pseudonym of the writer Amandine Aurore Lucile Dupin. She and Alfred de Musset, the romantic poet, fell in love in France and split up in Venice.

CHAPTER EIGHTEEN

Some Compassion for Sand and Musset!

Thus, Linda began to lament Musset's misadventures.
"O God, I wonder how he feels
He who looking for happiness finds sadness in an area
Where others experience, however, an infallible peace and a perfect idyll!
O God, what a quirk is this!
Pining after love, we find hatred!
And not only should we stay away from our joy, we are compelled to quit too!

Then, we miss the unrivaled glee which was ours when we came!
Then, sorry and shot, we go back home!
Then, we stop dreaming about mountains and wonders!
Then, we become helpless and lose our mind!
And we would like to die!
And we would like to arm ourselves and go to war against the abductor!
Against that demon!

And we would like to get our sweetheart back from that place
Like Helen from Troy[36]!
And at this time, the song which we sing is a mournful one!
It is like a funeral song which farewells our dead parent!

Ah! What a staggering blow in the city,
Where a husband looking for happiness,
Should one evening see desperately his wife in love with someone else!
That is the hardship through which
Alfred de Musset went when losing his sweetheart here!"

---

[36] The Trojan War is told by Homer in the Iliad. According to that legend, it would have exploded over Helen, wife of Menelaus, king of Sparta, after she was allegedly abducted by Paris son of Priam, king of Troy.

"When she left Musset," Alberto said,
"With his primary care doctor she felt in love here!
However, let us admit that this disciple of Hippocrates
Did not have in mind to take the poet's wife!
George Sand that beautiful lady was the one
Who made the first step toward that love affair!

In the beginning, the doctor feigned indifference to her passion.
He ignored whatever she did to conquer his heart.
By the time, the hapless poet on his hospital bed
Ignored that his doctor was also his rival!

"Tell me why Sand betrayed the man who loved her so much!" Adele asked.
Tell me how come she left him!
I don't think that her misconduct should be motivated by greed
Or by any kind of ambition to become famous!
For before she met the physician, Sand was already a celebrity!
As a novelist and a history teller,
It is unthinkable that she should look for fame in such a relationship!

"We should not pitilessly set that learned woman in the pillory
Because she came to Venice and betrayed her man that way! " Andrea said.
In fact, she and Musset coming to Italy expected to find in that place
A way to strengthen their affective link and to protect their love against chitchats!
Then Sand older than him condescended to follow him here despite all odds.
Does not her sacrifice mean that she could stay with him forever?

Oh, friends, moving to Venice should have cost a lot to her!
Not only did she accept to follow him to Italy,
She also left behind wealth, property, and children!
And I will not mention her difficult journey to Italy
Nor will I talk of her failing health during her travel.
But all this sacrifice which she accepted
Could prove how much she loved Musset
Like a sincere woman who supports her husband in everything."

"She made that sacrifice for the happiness of a dear companion!" Joshua said.
"In fact, what won't do a wife for the man whom she really loves?
What wouldn't she do for him when her heart incessantly beats for him?
What wouldn't she do for him when believing in his sincerity?
What wouldn't she do for him when love makes her go on her knees?
Tell me what a woman will not exchange against a sincere love
When the lover excels in tenderness?"

"Those questions are worth our attention as we ponder over them." Adele said.
Whether you are rich or poor, when you are in love,
You deny yourself for the sake of the loved one.
You are ready to follow him wherever he may go!
Should he run away, you want to flee with him!
Should you leave your parents, you want to leave with him!
You can even jeopardize our own life for the sake of him!
To protect him against a natural disaster!
You can even sell all your goods in order to feed him!
And when we love someone, we condone his weaknesses and oppose his enemies!
When we fall in love with someone, we give him happiness, tenderness, and riches!
We promise earth and moon, eternal faithfulness."

And then Alberto said,
"When you love a woman just as we love water,"
You give yourself to her!
But if she doubts about you, she will undo all things
To find a truthful love, the only one thing which women really need!
Like a bird which at night, finding a tree rests on its branch."

"Let's go back a while to the faithless lady." Adele continued.
"Sometimes we oppose Sand as we take the side of the betrayed poet
Whom however she loved!
In fact, at the peak of his suffering,
The poet of "*Les Nuits*" and of "*Le Pelican*" moves our heart!
Nevertheless, I am inclined to think
That Musset should have done something which hurt her feeling.

In that hypothesis, losing confidence in Musset,
Sand would stop loving him to fall in love with Dr. Pagello!
If any event must have an explanation,
Their breakup can also find here its own, I think.
Then we can more likely end all unjust comments
When knowing which one of the two lovers made the first step.
That's why to be honest with you,
I just want to appreciate the consequences of their misadventure,
Which no one can deny!
The great beneficiary is Literature
Upon which both lovers called to pour out their hearts!
"Lélia[37]" and "Lorenzacio[38]" and other artworks by these writers entertain all!

Alas! It is at the cost of the poets' suffering that poetry blossoms
And that the readers have a good time
Reading about their worst disappointments!
How many like Musset sob and cry for a fickle woman or for a defunct one?
Whatever the cause, O Poet, your word,
From the language of mourning only you borrow it!
So did Lamartine deploring of Elvire
The unexpected departure to the unknown places!
Thus do all delirious hearts who grieve their distress through their lines!"

After all, the guests led the conversation to others having sung an unhappy love
Until they stopped speaking of writers and quitted the table at night;
But all was not over.
For Mme Alberto still had another beautiful surprise for the guests,
A surprise which Linda stills remembers:
Andrea began to play piano.
And at each piece which she executed, O God,
All eyes were wet with tenderness tears!
And Alberto, so proud of his beautiful princess
Drew close to her and then gave her a kiss!

---

[37] *Lélia* (1833) a novel by Sand.
[38] *Lorenzaccio* (1834) a Tragedy by Musset.

CHAPTER NINETEEN

O Venice, How Old Are You?

The next day, Linda almost swooned over Venice's attraction.
She could not help personifying the city
Like the poet Lamartine talking to Milly, his birthplace
Whose hills and mountains he had longed for!

"Oh Venice, tell me please how old you are!
You whom the plastic arts have always made younger!
Please, remind me of the great-barbarian conquests
Which your coquettish soul had witnessed long ago
In your joyful days as well as in your gloomy time!

What Kings, what emperors, and what celebrities
Seduced by your beauty have sailed on your waters?
How many love songs, Venice, haven't you heard
From these who continue titillating your ears
From these who every day, fascinated with you
Have sung barcarolles to your delighted waves?

Oh! How they have made you witness their honeymoon
Wherever they come from!
Whether they come from far or from a nearby shore,
They make you the reward of their so faithful love!
While you, so happy, provide them in return
With an endless souvenir for their gleeful marriage!

Did you really provoke the tears of Hannibal[39]?
When the latter, compelled to give up the Italy,
Went his way with nothing! Went back to *Carthago*!
And then proposed a truce to the famous Scipio[40]
A truce which rejected that Roman dictator!
O Venice, were you well an infant at that time?

When of the Vesuvius the shimmering crater
In its cinerary waves plunged the Latin cities,
How many did flee to your shores, O Venice?
How many you saw within your enclosure,
Who seeking oblivion in your quiet bosom,
Actually got appeased by your light-gentle wind?

Oh! How old were you when Licius Catiline[41]
Through his conspiracy disturbed the Roman State
And that of Cicero the famous rhetoric
Claimed his life as well as this of his assistants?
Tell me! Were you a child at that time, O Venice!
When these connivers faced their sad execution?

---

[39] During the Second Punic War, Hannibal, commanding general of the Carthaginian army had won two great victories over the Romans, one at Trasimeno (217 BC) and one in Cannes (216 BC). The defeated Romans, worrying about the Roman hegemony, appointed the young Scipio Africanus dictator. Unlike his predecessor, the Roman general Fabius Maximus who had preferred to face the Carthaginian army in Italy, Scipio Africanus decided on carrying the war into the enemy territory, in Africa. Upon seeing the Roman army at Carthage's doors, the frightened Carthaginians recalled Hannibal from Italy. Then compelled to leave the Italian territory that his army had been treading for years, Hannibal would shed tears of regret.

[40] The Roman general Publius Cornelius Scipio (236-283) received the nickname Africanus after his victory over Hannibal at Zama (202 BC), a victory which ended the Second Punic War.

[41] Catilina's conspiracy against the Roman Republic was denounced by Cicero *in his "Against Catiline"*.

Oh how old were you? When Emperor Valerian[42]
Fell like a scoundrel into the barbarian hands?
He who sent to their grave many Christ's followers!
He who always treated those martyrs with disdain!
He who liked seeing them always persecuted
Wherever they met them, even in catacombs!

When female luxury in the Roman city
Irritated Cato who then being consul
Managed to outlaw all their extravagance,
When their orgy threatened the matrimonial bonds,
In both the patricians' and plebeians' classes
O Venice, did you find their conduct harmful too?

And when they committed the most scandalous crime
Through which they killed the Christ, our blameless redeemer,
When all his followers faced their end everyday
As a hobby offered to the Roman City,
Tell me! Did you condone all those misdeeds on earth?
Or did you take pity on the innocent ones?

Tell me how you could if in this ancient time,
Before the beginning of the Gothic conquests
You did not exist yet anywhere on the map?
Maybe can all the land in which you had been born
Answer all those questions and teach your visitors
Before happy with you, they can then take their leave!

Of course, you can tell them you saw the agony
Of the Roman Empire ending in infamy!
You can tell them how the terror of the earth
Kept struggling despite all in the Byzantine land
After it was buried in its old western part!

---

[42]   Emperor Valerian (253-260)AD, a ferocious persecutor of the Jesus' followers.

Please, tell them how much you had fought to save it
And how much you saw vainly your blood pour
To keep it from dying over there every day!
As your defeated sons falling back to yourself
Bewailed over his end which no one could avoid!

Sure, tell them you had seen, O Venice, your galleys
Sadly sinking in these pitiless Crusades
And your sailors leaving without coming back,
Whether they fell under pagan- barbarian swords,
Sources of inspiration for songs and for epics,
Or died as shipwrecked ones!

After you eye-witnessed the collapse of the empire
What lesson would you like to teach to the humans?
Let them know, I beg you, that nothing eternal
Can come from the mortals who all should go their way!
And that on earth they will leave nothing but their trace
As did once and the poor and the rich early men!

And let them know that all those swallowed up in death,
Either the civilized or the barbarian have had all the same end!
And that time did not take pity on the Roman knights
Nor did it feel sorry for slaves and Sicarians
And that only the martyrs wrapped in their shrouds
Aspired to emerge from nothingness by thousands!

CHAPTER TWENTY

Linda Misses her Two Wedlock Sons

Night was very serene, and in every single Island,
Motionless had stood the Venetian transportation system.
Linda, like Joshua, back to their luxurious hotel slept like a log.
Usually, after a long excursion,
She went to bed early up to around nine o'clock in the morning!
In that day, however, by unfortunate exception
She woke up before dawn all of a sudden!
She had been snatched from her deep sleep by a terrible dream:
Immersed in her sleep in Venice,
She had seen her more handsome-wedlock boy
Struggling in the arms of a kidnapper in Turgeau!
That was the dreadful spectacle that woke up her.

Right away, she jumped from her bed and desperately gave the nanny a call.
Happily! She got a very-good news regarding her two legitimate sons
Who were said to be safe and secure in their bed!
Then Linda realized how her dream had misled her!
However, since frightened Linda had already woke up the husband too,
She told him about the scary images which she had seen.

On his part, Joshua, who did not believe in dreams at all, ached from laughing.
"Oh, disturbed wife," he said, "forgive my laughing so hard at you!
Your dream did not foreshadow anything!
It was not worth being that scare nor spending that horrific moment for nothing!"

"Why are you talking like that, Honey?" Linda asked.
"Are you skeptical to such a point that you underestimate the message of God
Who puts us on the alert by means of a dream?"

"O Wife, are you crazy!" Joshua exclaimed.

"I won't marvel at your viewpoint anyway!

For, like you, many have believed in such things with the same exaggeration!

Unfortunately, they have failed to know that today there is no point in doing so.

To tell the truth, only long ago, our Creator

Resorted to dreams to provide well-partial details about events to happen on earth!

In that remote past, profitable or harmful for many, these images came from God.

And they came true as predicted!"

"And what about today, Honey?" Linda asked in turn.

"Has our immutable and loving God stopped talking to us the same way?

Has He stopped sending us similar messages to protect us from dangers?"

"What you asked me had been already done!" Joshua said.

"In fact, the Bible, the flawless book,

Already tells us of everything to happen in the future!

We just need to read in it, carefully, and know about what to do

As we are longing for the oncoming judgment time!

Long ago, when God had spoken to the humans through dreamlike means,

He did not fulfill his prophetic work relating to earth and to its future.

Later, when he was done with it,

He told his prophets about everything to come soon!

For the present, with the Bible being complete,

Men no longer need a dream to know about the divine plan.

Thus, it is pointless to bother yourself about your dreamlike images!

And you waste your time, Honey, thinking that God is talking to you that way!

"If true, Sweetie," Linda continued,

"Could it be that my dream came from a different source than my unique God?

Or should we consider our dreams to be aimless?"

"History has shown that apart from the God of Israel," he said,
"Other spirits resorted to dreams to communicate with the humans too!
Obviously, this is where the shoe pinches.
For example, some writers report that among the Amerindians
Supernatural messages used to haunt the dreams of both men and women
Who then knew nothing about the Bible!
And following the same source,
Those natives always looked for the meaning of those dreams
Coming from the spiritual world!

In *The Iliad*, tale by Homer, Greek poet,
An Olympian god informed Agamemnon, the King of the Greeks,
That he could without fear gather his army and go victoriously to war!
Now what about the account narrated in *the Anabasis?*
Allow me to support my thesis by referring to this account too.
In that story, Xenophon thrived to highlight for the readers
How dreams saved him and his army desperately trapped in an unknown land!

Chapter Twenty-One

The Dreams of Xenophon

"Honey, you always come up with a series of historical facts
In order to support your argument! Don't you?"
"Of course, Baby!" Joshua replied.
"I can't wait for you to tell me about Xenophon's dreams!" Linda continued.
"After Xerxes[43] died," Joshua said,
"His two sons, Artaxerxes and Cyrus the Younger were fighting over the throne.
Artaxerxes, who had legally succeeded to his father as the older son,
Was wrongly apprised of a conspiracy
Which his little brother, Cyrus the Younger, would have woven against him!
For that reason, Artaxerxes wanted to execute his little brother. In that circumstance, no need to say
How the Younger, feared for his threatened life
Although, in reality, he did not covet the position of his older brother at all!
What a pity! Tissaphernes his own friend!
Wrongly accused him of plot against the royalty!
Therefore, rightly this treason dismayed the innocent-younger brother!
Worse yet, if their mother, Queen Parysatis failed
To intercede quickly for him with Artaxerxes,
Actually, the Younger would be killed!

However, after Cyrus the Younger was bailed out,
He went back to this post and summoned his troops from all the kingdoms
In which he had a countless number of partisans!
Greeks, barbarians, mercenaries, and all strongmen,
Who agreed to follow him in war, then joined him!
He constituted an army amounting to ten thousand souls about!
And since he preferred his Greek allied for their heroism than the others

---

[43]   According to Xenophon's account in *The Anabasis*, it was well Darius II Xerxes who ruled the Persian Empire 423-405 BC.

He enrolled important Hellenic squadrons
Which he placed under the commandment of his most famous generals such as
Aristippus, Xenia, Clearchus, Socrates of Achaea, and Xenophon!
The latter was the witness who reported that event in his *Anabasis*[44]!

The Younger's army grew up as long as, crossing the cities,
He enrolled new soldiers.
He also relied on huge-naval forces, which could match his brother's fleet!

Upon hearing about his little brother landing with his troops in Babylon,
Artaxerxes marched against him with his royal army.
But The Younger was the first who distinguished him among his soldiery!
Suddenly, the little brother fled towards him,
And with a unprecedented rage,
He assaulted Artaxerxes across his breastplate and left him for dead!
However, in the meantime,
The Younger was killed with an arrow that reached him in his face!

Honey, the Younger's death went unnoticed to his own soldiers.
And after his troops knew it a while later,
They felt so disappointed!
And despite their martial excellence, they vainly tried to avenge him!
Moreover, having lost some good soldiers in the battlefield,
They had to act urgently!
Then anarchic and amounting to ten thousand souls only,
The defeated army could no longer stay calm in a hostile and unknown territory,
For their victorious enemy might anytime come back and treat them like captives!
Consequently, they felt the need of a new leader
Who should relieve them of their cruel deception!
Bring them back to their homeland!
Help them to survive their hunger and their lack of water
And to stay alive despite the great shortage

---

[44]   Historical work By Xenophon.

That already cost them many horses!
Above all, the new leader had to boost their military morale
That was so lowered by that loss!
In fact, who did not believe in Cyrus the Younger?
After Xerxes died, the greatest part of the empire
Wished the Younger were the one to succeed to his father!
Even Parysatis, his mother,[45] would want him to the new king!
So after he decided on fighting against his brother,
He found across the high Asia Persian kings to pay his troops
And to provide them with other forms of support!
And even prior to crossing the Euphrates towards Babylon
Where death awaited him, he was warmly welcomed as the victorious rival.
Moreover, many royal soldiers deserting Artaxerxes' army joined him!
They placed more interest in his reign than in his brother government.

That's why, at the beginning of the battle,
The optimistic Greek troops sang with jubilation their paean of victory!
They realized that their dream nearly came true!
However the reverse of the situation swiftly changed their hope into distress!

"Across that dismay," Linda said, "could you tell me
Whom they chose as leader to help them quit these dangerous areas
And bring them back to Greece and to cheer them up?
Please, tell me on whom they relied to make themselves survive successfully!"

"Following Xenophon in *The Anabasis*[46]," Joshua answered,
"It was at this phase that dream came to play an instrumental role
In the survival of these troops!
At night, just after he had pondered over the situation,
Xenophon got asleep and contemplated a dreamlike image.

---

[45] According to Xenophon, Parysatis, their mother, who preferred Cyrus the younger than her older son, always saw in that one the future heir of the throne. We understand that she could not help obtaining from ArtaXerxes the release of her second-beloved son without alacrity!

[46] Work by Xenophon, Greek historian, disciple of Socrates.

A scary spectacle he seemed to have seen:
A lightning would fall on his paternal house,
It was the message which he had received!
An incredible communication, an ambiguous one!
To see that rapid fire falling down on his house!
What a sibylline oracle for him! I am telling you!
He felt so terrified by this enigmatic representation!

Most of the time, people are in trouble
When they take their dream for an important presage
And that they fail to decode the message that it keeps into hiding for them!
Then whether that image seemed to presage a good thing
Or foreshadow a horrifying blow for the dreamer or for anyone else,
It leaves them enormously concerned. And it was Xenophon's situation.

"At the height of anxiety, Xenophon, however, saw one more dream.
That one looked excellent to him, for it was more accurate
And seemed to be more appropriate to that actual circumstance.
That second image also seemed to revoke the first-confusing one.
In fact, in that dream, he was set free from a rope which had tied him up.

He considered such an image to be more likely a good omen.
Because it seemed to predict him the release of the defeated troops!
Hence, he did not hesitate
To tell his battlefield companions about such a message,
That had a soothing effect on their mind.

"Quickly, they realized that
Xenophon was the one designed through the dreams
To be the rescuing leader for whom they were looking.
And unanimously, they appointed him the head of their defeated armies
With the mission to command their troops in these critical time
At which they nearly surrendered.
And Xenophon conscious of his great-military ability accepted that post.
Comforted in his interpretation of the dream,
He ensured to fulfill his mission
With such a success that he saved his legions

By repatriating his comrades against winds and tides!
Thus, his dreams aided him in breaking the deadlock and saving his army!
Now the whole question is to know from whom the message came.

"Listen, Honey!" Linda exclaimed in turn.
"Maybe did Jehovah God talk to Xenophon too! You never know!
This Greek warrior could be the worshipper of the true God.
In that hypothesis, he might receive these dreamlike images
From the God of the Bible!
Did not the true God Himself have the pagan king Nebuchadnezzar
Dream about his temporary removal from his own throne?
Did not He cause that monarch to see the future- millenarian reign?
Did not the true God in that circumstance let the king know
He Jehovah alone is the originator of both the Heaven and the Earth?

Based on these facts, Honey,
I am inclined to believe that the true God spoke to Xenophon too
In order to protect the Greek army against
Any possible attack from Artaxerxes and to show to them their way home!
And to keep them alive in spite of their loss!
For now, Honey, do you still need to prove that the true God
May regardless of our beliefs send a dream to rescue us from dangers?
Should we doubt any more that the true God
Should still give that way his Holy decisions today?"

"Let us assume that you are right," the husband answered.
"In this event, why would the true God allow Cyrus the Younger to be killed?
And why would He grant the victory to the victorious camp
While helping the defeated one?
Why would not He put the Cyrus' troops on top of his brother's?
There is no doubt! Jupiter, or Apollo was the sender of those messages!

In fact, when Cyrus the Younger invited Xenophon to follow him in war,
The latter at the instigation of Socrates, his teacher, went to Delphi,
Where he consulted the oracles of the Olympian gods on Cyrus' expedition!
For the present, Honey, thrive to know that

Any dreams coming from Jehovah had to serve his purpose.
Whether these images appeared to his faithful worshipper, or to a pagan leader,
They always had to do with Jehovah's plan.
Sent by Jehovah, those dreams were linked to the Kingdom of God
To come to earth so soon at an appointed time!
It is the criterion that helps us identify the source of the dreams."

"However I don't believe that we need to question the origin of our dreams!
For a dream remains only a dream!" Linda said.
"For what should we identify relentlessly their source and their meaning?"

"We may have pointless dreams, in fact." The husband answered.
"As said, there are insignificant images deserving no real attention.
It is specific to humans to dream at night about what they had seen daytime.
In those dreams, they may even quench their real needs
Such as eating, drinking, or taking a ride.
Sigmund Freud[47], the father of the Psychoanalysis
Found these aspects to be inherent to the human life!

And as for the Bible, it speaks of the natural dreams too,
Of dreams which the humankind has had for centuries!
These dreams have been part of the sleep of the mortal ones.
Therefore, we can now take them lightly!
But as regards the premonitory messages,
We need to question ourselves when we get them.
For the true God no longer communicates his holy decisions by their means.
Hence, in case we receive such a communication, we should be careful!"

"As soon as I listen to you," Linda said,
I have no doubt about your great fear of supernatural dreams!
However, I would like to know why you want to stay away from such images

---

[47]   Sigmund Freud, the father of the psychoanalysis.

The same way you avoid lying on people and committing a murder!"

"For a simple reason," the husband answered.
In fact, dreams have made part in a spectrum of supernatural ways
By which the false gods draw close to the humans and obtain their worship.
In the history of occult practices,
So many people serving the false divinities
Have faced the obligation to appease those blood-thirsty demons
With odious sacrifices!
And most of the times,
How many children did not perish as vivid sacrifices offered to Baal
Or as victims offered by Hannibal?
Long ago, how many lost their lives on Aztec altars?
Long ago, how many human sacrifices were slaughtered by the Gallic druids?
How many had been sacrificed even in the allegedly civilized nations?

"Since the gods might demand these sacrifices by means of a dream too,
Would there be a good reason for us
To see the dreamlike messages with a positive eye?
One may argue that they are useful to people in trouble like Xenophon!
But their usefulness is nothing but a trick
To make the demons look friendly to us!
Initially, those spirits can offer their help through a dream.
And a naive person may trust them.
However, the follow-up is terrible! It is quite unwise
To bond friendships with the spiritual enemies of our loving- true God!
Because next to Him only, far from us are the ravages!
Far away from Him only are the human sacrifices claimed by false gods!
And the gods of Voodoo will run way from us!
And their sorcerers and their seers won't take any advantage of us!
Nor will we exchange our children against riches
Coming from wicked demons
Who promise a happiness which they do not have for themselves!
Because not only are they cursed spirits, they did not create anything!"

Thus had spoken the couple Trazileon in Italy!

At the same time, Jain still missed his mother in Port-au-Prince,
Which Linda in Venice ignored.
Although she made a phone call to her nanny to Turgeau,
She was never told by her maidservant
About anybody waiting for her nearby.
And that was the best decision, which Marianne had never made,
By keeping silent about the visitors of her traveling mistress!
For, even though Linda was partying in Italy every day,
Even though she seemed to be absolutely glad abroad,
She couldn't help worrying about her two wedlock-born sons
Whom she had left in Turgeau!

Who can ignore the fragility of a mother?
Of a mother who commingles joy and sadness
When she focuses her attention on her children
And that far away from them she feels restless?
Then she is looking forward to one thing only:
Coming back home to her children whom she had left behind!
This was, in fact, the meaning of Linda's dream.
Yet was the image which she had seen had been misleading.
By the time, Linda and her husband took good care of each other.
And she needed to be strong and patient in order to complete her vacation.

CHAPTER TWENTY-TWO

In San Marco Island

And time elapsed quickly. Shortly, Joshua and his wife had to leave Venice.
Then, they were making their very last excursion in San- Marco Island
Of which old constructions forced everyone's admiration!
In that occasion, a multi-racial crowd gathered to that place,
All of them curious fans of the Fine Arts!

The couple Trazileo had crossed some of them in Florence.
And once again by a happy coincidence, they met them in that touristic site
In which all visitors in awe of the old buildings were socializing with one another.
By the time, they led their conversations to the beautiful Gothic[48] style.
And one of them asked,
"How come artworks contribute so much to the success of tourism any where?"

That question aroused to its climax the interest of everyone.
It led to a symposium in behalf of all famous architects, painters, and sculptors
Whether they had cultivated the classical or the baroque[49] art,
Or had been trained by the masters of Milan,
Whether they had attended the Umbrian school[50]
Or had followed the Florentine artists,

---

[48] In the Middle Ages, especially in the period between the twelfth and fourteenth century, they used the word *Gothic* in a pejorative sense to describe the artistic style of the Goths and Germans regarded by the Romans as barbarians and uncivilized. However, the Gothic art was to assert its dominance increasingly in religious and secular areas after the fall of the Roman Empire.

[49] The baroque art is recognizable by its bizarre and spectacular appearance.

[50] The Umbrian school played an important role in Italy during the Renaissance art.

Whether they had been influenced by the Romanticists[51] or by the Cubists[52],

And regardless of whom those artists had followed:

Naturalists[53] or impressionists[54],

And even though they should come very late to the plastic arts,

Even though they should be attached to the rococo[55] style,

All noteworthy artists indistinctly were remembered in that conversation.

And Joshua Trazileo was found to be the first to answer that question.

"Without the artworks, I think,

There would be few journeyers to tour joyfully the World!" He said.

"And there would not be so many sightseers

To explore even this beautiful country which we are treading today!

In fact, many visiting a foreign location would like to keep it in memory.

But how can they do so if there is nothing in that site to capture their attention?

They will just leave it without thinking of revisiting it in the future!

But the situation can be different, I think, if they find in any visited places

Some artwork evoking the conquests of the welcoming nation,

Or if they discover an artistic achievement reflecting its various realities;

However, many wrongly think that monumental arts

Are only meant to adorn the cities

And to charm tourists coming to Marseille, to Seville, or to Luxembourg!

In reality, does the usefulness of the monumental arts

---

[51]   In visual arts, the Romantics in the name of individual freedom, have expressed in their artistic creation their inner self, their own dreams and their own passions.

[52]   This artistic movement that took place within the first two decades of the 20th century was advocated by the painters Georges Braque and Pablo Picasso. These artists preferred geometric figures such as cube, rectangle, pyramid, circle than the pictorial forms of the Renaissance.

[53]   In painting as in literature, Naturalism (1880-1890) aimed at the faithful and genuine representation of the realities of daily life.

[54]   The Impressionist artists (1872-1886) were fixed as goals to paint the changing and shifting landscapes illuminated by air or by light.

[55]   The rococo style is inspired in part by the Baroque and is featured as well by extravagant decorations.

Uniquely consist in the ornament of a town?
In other terms, do the plastic arts aim simply to build splendid villas?
Erect palaces with exciting façades?
Paint one hundred mural frescoes and decorate towers?
Is it quite simply the genius which some men have
To carve a heroic face out of a stone?
To populate the beautiful parks and public squares with busts, with statues
Representing either an animal, or a human?
To draw up false gods in carnal forms
In a Nirvana, or in the paradise, or to describe an eternal fire
Where condemned ones are purging themselves as the legend shows it?

No, I do not think that the mission of the plastic arts is fulfilled this way only."

"Of course the plastic arts", Linda added,
"Do more than embellishing public places!
They do more than charming the transient tourists.
Architects, painters, and sculptors
All of them, in fact, have influenced the evolution of the civilization!
They have all caused noteworthy changes like the writers in the phonetic[56]
arts!·

Who can ignore the writers' contributions to the triumph of the Human rights?
For example Rousseau, Diderot, and Voltaire [57]
Are credited with denouncing the abuses of a sitting system on slavery;

---

[56]   The arts are divided into visual arts and phonetic arts. The visual arts such as painting, architecture, sculpture are expressed in space by means of forms and colors. The phonetic arts such as music, literature are expressed in time with the sounds.

[57]   Rationalist philosophers Voltaire, Rousseau, Diderot and Montesquieu had prepared the French Revolution through their ideas.

They are also attributed with provoking through their works[58]
The end of the feudal regime once taken in disgust!
Today, if all people without distinctions of color, race, sex, and religion
Are considered being born equal in rights,
If all have the same right to defense, they owe those writers such benefits!

Similarly, plastic arts at some points have contributed to enormous changes
Involving more than adorning public places;
Long ago, the Church[59] used the plastic arts against paganism.
Then she made them a didactic instrument to teach the Bible.

Indeed, after the Roman Empire had fallen,
The Church culturally became the powerful heiress of Rome.
She was so proud of that legacy that she thrived to rebuild the defunct empire.
She wanted Rome, nicknamed the *Eternal city,*
To be back on her feet as the *City of God,* free from opprobrium and heinous sins;
And to rebuild Rome as a sacrosanct and sinless city,
The Church relied on the plastic arts to teach about the thought of God!
Thus through their works,
The artists were expected to tell of God, of His personality, and of His plan.
They had to show what kind of worship God accepts for good
And which way He deals with his own worshippers.

Since Architecture was use to that end,
The ecclesial buildings have ascended toward the heaven
And captured the universal attention by their glitzy sparkles
So much so that visitors, whether they were Persian or Mede,

---

[58]   We owe the 1789 Revolution to the awareness resulting from the anti-feudal ideas conveyed by works such as the Spirit of the Laws, The Persian Letters (Montesquieu), The Philosophical Letters, Zadig, Candide (Voltaire), Speech on the Arts and Sciences, The Discourse on Inequality, The Social Contract (Rousseau) etc.

[59]   It is reported that Constantine the Great, who defended Christianity against paganism, assigned to the artists of his time the mission to tell the holy history through the visual arts such as architecture, painting, and sculpture.

They came to swoon over the architectural beauty of the Church everywhere!
They came to admire the enchanting exploits of both painters and carvers
Outside and inside the Church
Where people have worshiped God as a Trinity[60]!

And the tourists came to the Italian land.
They came to other Christian countries as well.
They came anywhere the Church extended her crown
To admire the architectural achievements in remembrance of Rome
And of her great fame!

Furthermore, in the hands of the famous Church,
The plastic arts have boosted the economy of the country
Where the ancient- ecclesiastical construction is also a factor
On which the officials rely to promote tourism.
After all, we have to ask ourselves
Whether or not these artworks have reflected the will of God in reality!
And whether these artistic realizations have conveyed
A real disgust for paganism[61]!

"In fact, it is by faith, not by sight that we can worship our celestial Father.
Whether we adore Him or not in a splendid construction,
He will accept our offerings if and only if
We follow his commandments and make his Holy word our unique guide.
For He hates seeing the true cult mixed with exogenous things!
However in the Middles Ages,
Not only did the Church adopt the Aristotelian[62] ethics,
She commingled it with the Biblical teaching." And Joshua continued,

---

[60]   The Bible does not teach Trinity.

[61]   Some historians believe that the Church owes much to paganism on liturgical level, architectural, legal, and political. For example, Will Durant in The Story of Civilization Part III wrote, " The Christian Church followed the footsteps of the Roman state."

[62]   In medieval times, the philosophy of Aristotle, Greek philosopher, disciple of Plato, has integrated the Catholicism on the initiative of Thomas Aquinas, Italian theologian and doctor of the Church.

"To assess the contributions of plastic arts to tourism,
We should not focus on the Church only!
The sightseers visiting Europe are attracted by secular works as well,
No matter whether they tread a Castilian land, or a Venetian area,
Or any locations, where survives the remnant of a medieval castle,
In which the lords in spite of their social prestige had once led a boring
existence! If we go to Versailles, to the Luxembourg, or to any other cities,
We can admire non-ecclesiastical artworks which make the pride of the
artist too.

In reality, during the Italian Renaissance, the artists had discovered the
Antiquity
Of which charms and beauty they wanted to acquaint the public with.
And since they came to realize
That the Ancient Greeks and Romans had been better in everything,
They undertook to renew the latter's civilization.
Therefore, they dropped off the medieval philosophy with its ascetic views:

During the Middle-Ages and under the influence of its scholastic[63]
concepts,
It had been thought that wisdom consisted
Of despising the finest pleasures and bullying one's body.
They also thought that
Wisdom meant to extinguish one's physical desire and stifle one's passion.

Consequently, during the Renaissance,
The medieval conception proved to be obsolete.
The artists plunged their look into the Antiquity
Whose myths and philosophy exposed in the humanities[64]
Better fit to their quest for earthly happiness!

In that context, the plastic arts found a new partnership in humanism
To which it became necessary to show

---

[63] Scholastic relates to scholasticism, a philosophical and theological system, which
   in the Middle Ages commingled the Aristotelian ethics with the teachings, the
   dogmas, and the tradition of the Church.
[64] The classical works.

How beautiful the Greco-Roman civilization had been, in reality,
And how people could enjoy it again!
Once resuscitated by the humanists[65],
The Greco-Roman civilization became the inspiring source of the artists
Who got to know about it from the ancients books once ignored!
In the aftermath of the fall of Constantinople[66],
The survivors of the Ottoman war, fleeing to Italy,
Brought the ancient books with them!
And the invention of the printing,
Will all make those ancient works more accessible to people.
The readers came to discover the Greek and Roman legends
Hence, Olympian[67] gods have invaded the mural frescoes, the tableaus
And other painting works telling about a classical- fairy tale!
Since then, Olympian deities have filled the museums
And have lived as humans in a pagan setting."
It should take much more time, would be, to say how ended the debate,
The last one in which Joshua and his wife took part in Venice
Just before they got ready to fold their luggage and take their leave.

---

[65] In the Renaissance era, humanists advocated the study of the Greek and Latin texts.

[66] Constantinople, the capital city of the eastern-Roman empire was known to have the greatest library of the Greco-Roman Antiquity. But in 1453 AD, the Ottoman Turks conquered Constantinople and renamed it Istanbul. During that battle, Byzantine survivors fled to Italy with lots of Greek and Roman books.

[67] In Greek mythology, Mount Olympus was the abode of the gods.

CHAPTER TWENTY-THREE

To the Egyptian Land

In Port-au-Prince, lonely Jain pined after his mother, Linda,
Who on her part missed only her wedlock sons,
As the unique object of her maternal love!
Unaware of Jain's grief, Linda extended her vacation abroad
And took a ride with her husband to the Egyptian land!
The couple had just left the Venetian gondoliers behind.
In several days, they would be landing in Cairo as previewed.
Traveling in Africa had remained a longtime dream to them,
And one of their most beautiful project in their existence!
They had dreamed about it so relentlessly!
By now, they were heading for the land that attracted them so much!
They expected to tread that land where their ancestors had lived long ago!
A continent which yesterday had seen so many masters in the World
Succeed at its expenses!
For wow on board their ship
They craved for landing in that land around which one hundred stories
turn!
They longed for admiring in it
Anything, which their race had formerly made by its own!
However, prior to discovering the places whence came their ebony skin,
They would be celebrating on board for days!
They would have a good time together from Venice to Athens!
They would make a stop in the country of Socrates[68].
After that, they would continue their trip by departing from the port of
Piraeus[69]
Until they cross in Mediterranean[70] for their oriental tour.
And as elated travelers, they had been sailing for four days

---

[68] This Greek philosopher was born in Athens in 470 BC.
[69] It is the largest port in all of Greece.
[70] From Venice to the Egyptian land, the ship was expected to sail in the Adriatic
      and in the Ionian seas and to finish its crossing in the Mediterranean.

Craving for happiness over and over,
Singing, dancing, playing, and absolutely worriless!
No one could find enough words to describe their joy on the sea!
Nor could no one tell enough about their jubilation on the wonderful water!

The Adriatic Sea[71], then, was torn
Under their craft roaring and poking fun at the waves
As much as at the fishermen who were dropping their nets and their fishing hooks!
Evenings and mornings had elapsed when the ship got access to the Ionian waters
And that it had left the Italian peninsula behind from a long distance!

They felt at home on board *The Adriatic Dawn*
In which they were enjoying a romantic ambiance.
The crew members ensured that all passengers received an impeccable service!
And treated like princes, Joshua and Linda forgot about everything!
I mean they forgot even about Port-au-Prince, distant city then!

Guess who were with them on board among so many journeyers?
Guess who were sailing to the East with them!
The couples Alberto and Andrea, Christian, and Christine!
How many tourists were on board?
Two thousand and twenty-three travelers
Including people of different sexes, ages, races and languages!
Attica reserved to these errant visitors
The remains of the gods, their statues, and their temples
And the Acropolis of which vestiges the visitors were eager to explore!
Attica welcomed everyone to its shore,
Those who had never seen its sunrise

---

[71] While sailing in the Adriatic Sea from Venice to Athens, the journeyers will have the whole peninsula of Italy on their right and the countries of the Balkan Europe (Croatia, Bosnia and Herzegovina, Montenegro and others) to the left until they reach the Ionian Sea where the port of Piraeus is located on the left.

And who by going from seaboard to seaboard would never see a similar one again!
Maybe would they go if they had enough time
And discover the Cyclades, or the Ionian Islands which are so beautiful shat
We must leave them against our own will and dream about them later!

CHAPTER TWENTY-FOUR

Hello, Athens!

To the harbor of Piraeus
The cruise arrived then.
Fully playful, so the passengers sang:

"Hi, Land of Athens,
What a kind wind
Is this bringing us tour your city today!

Oh! Attica, please!
Deign to welcome all our brothers
Who, fleeing from their boredom, drop by here to have
fun!

May our short presence
On your enchanting ground
Bring more joy to our hearts!

Moved by your charming past,
We would like to search
Your faithful memory for more than one event!

For all which we have heard
About the Persian[72] wars
Which you faced long ago!
For the historical scene
Whence the King Darius[73],

---

[72] In the fifth century BC, the Persian Wars broke out between the Greeks and
Persians also called Medes. The Greeks were the winners.
[73] Darius I, the father of Xerxes I.

Flew once from Marathon[74]!

For the scene where Xerxes
Sometime at Salamis
Lost the battle in front of your so brave squadrons!

And for the site in which
Median army in Plataea
Raised its flags and was exterminated!

Could you show us the Acropolis
Witness of this past
At which the mankind attended your school!

Show us, please, your museums
In which are exposed your gods
Long ago created by imagination!

Where was the Areopagus?
Where your proud talkers
Dressed as wise men came and stood forth?

We mean this Areopagus
At which Apostle Paul
Bluntly spoke of the true God?

Show us the Agora
Where the Athenian city
Came and listen to Socrates, or to Demosthenes!

---

[74] 69 In the year 490 BC, the Athenian army commanded by General Miltiades won a runaway victory over the Persians. At the height of his elation, Miltiades sent the swiftest runner of his army, the Greek Philippides, to apprise the Athenians of the glorious event. The messenger hardly had time to transmit the news that he had already fallen dead after running 42 kilometers.

CHAPTER TWENTY-FIVE

Through Athens

All the visitors were given a cicerone to walk them across the Athenian
City.
Linda and her friends, however, needed no guide
Because Alberto and Andrea had got used to coming there so frequently!
The Venetian couple then went ahead fearlessly, like their escorts.
In fact, there was no danger from the population full of civility!
Thus the strangers could with peace of mind
Tour the country from city to city and enjoy Greek foods and drinks,
Admire orchards and meadows,
Get to Syndagma national park, a real paradise in summer time,
Come into contact with fascinating- botanic gardens
That make the attraction of the public square!
Mingle with the daily routine of Kifissia downtown
Where Greece with her charming face enticed the visitors
To enjoy life anywhere:
In the shops where they could buy anything!
At the restaurants where the culinary art
Was honored as a way to delight in the terrestrial life!
Everywhere at an amazing opera concert
That had them forget about the true hell[75]!

They could set sail to the Cyclades Islands
Of which attraction inspired feverish getaways,
Whether they visited the Lesbos Island
Or made an escape to Mount Athos,
In fact, they had been there!
They had been going to and fro,
To the amazement of Joshua and Linda!

---

[75]   This word comes from the Greek Hades which means, not a place of eternal
torment, but grave, cemetery.

Ah! What a great show to never miss!
When they saw from Athens the first sunrays announcing the day
Either behind the Hymettus Mountain
Or behind the heights of the Crete Island,
Or when they saw the solar furnace gradually blowing from the East
And reflecting on the sea with thousand firing rays
While in the Aegean Sea and in the countless Islands
The night was already gone as much as the half-light!

CHAPTER TWENTY-SIX

Linda Unveils Her Poetic Dream

The vessel had been anchored to the Athenian sea for three days.
Then, all the travelers remembered the order of the captain
To be back at time to the ship
So they could leave the wharf at the appointed time.
Nevertheless, many without saying it
Would like to stay a while longer in the City
In order to explore more adjacent islands!
As for Linda, she was so excited that
She could not help disclosing her major dream!
Of what did it consist in reality?

She had planned to publish her poetic work
Of which manuscript she had left at home.
For now, on board,
Not only did she talk about her goal in front of all,
She exposed both her literary creed and her poetic views!

"Could you tell us about the themes of your poetry?" Alberto asked her.
"Like many writers, did you deal with the Greek civilization in your lines?"
Then, Linda answered as follows,
"I don't intend to boast myself about my verses which carry a message for many.
Instead, I want to please all my readers
By sharing their joy and their disappointments!
I address my lines to these who experience a successful-happy love
As much as to these who suffer from a romantic failure.
I dedicate all my poetry to they who grieve the loss of their dear ones,
They who, focusing hopelessly on their ordeal,
Feel exhausted and lifeless!
That's why I borrowed from some literary schools
Their perennial art which has caught the attention
Of all those whom poetry motivates and consoles!

Far away from me too the bragging attitude of those
Who, proclaiming their poetic genius,
Think that they are exempt of criticism!
Actually, I am looking for a sincere appreciation from everyone!
Could you assess my lines, please?
Could you constantly submit my work to an honest examination?
Your fair judgments will not hurt me!
Please, refrain from seeking me atop the Parnassus Mount
Where they claim to find the masters of the poetic art!
It seems to me that I came too late to climb those heights.
Nor will you look for me on the Helicon peak,
The dwelling which the legend assigns to poetry!

Please, keep me far from the pretention to go up to that mountain!
However, even though I don't believe in the fairy tales, which
Exposed to a pagan society the mythic exploits of the Olympian gods,
I acknowledge the ancient poetry both for its oldness and its fictiveness.

"To talk honestly, I bear Epicurus a grudge
Since he taught that all in the universe comes from the inert atoms
Without a God, creator of the angels and the men!
Originator of the heaven and of the earth!

"I also oppose Epicurus' teaching that upon completing its natural cycle,
Everything in the universe should dissolve into matter,
Or disintegrate forever!

"If true there is not a God in whom I hope,
A God who created the World and these atoms,
How could these minuscule bodies
Design this beautiful universe without His Divine brain?
How could they conceive the plants, the animals, and the human kind?
For that reason, I invite anyone who actually grants credit to such an opinion
To screen it all the times and see how it opposes their common sense.

May you do that too?
You who make the universe spring to the existence by an amazing accident!
Could you do that too?
You who believe that men had evolved from an animal species by a certain time!
I think that it is not worth thriving to support this unbelievable idea.
For I do not believe that men come from a species of monkeys!

Thus you future readers of my poetry,
Please, try to understand the raison why
I have consulted those who since the antiquity
Have influenced so many religions by their own erroneous views!

CHAPTER TWENTY-SEVEN

Linda and the Greco Roman Myth

Linda was warmly praised orally and by hands clapping as well.
On his part, Joshua overwhelmed with surprise will stay amazed for long!
He had never seen his sweetheart talking of poetry before,
What about of her literary work?

As for Andrea, she felt so glad in that circumstance
That she invited other journeyers to join the literary circle.
"Are you done with your presentation, Linda?" Andrea asked.
"I would like to hear more about your poetic work!"
And Linda continued:
"Long ago, a lot of angels fell in love with beautiful women on earth.
Trying to enjoy carnal pleasure,
They came down and went into relationship with those females
 As reported in the Bible[76]!
However, through their fairy tales, Homer[77] and Hesiod[78] speak of false gods
Who would contract matrimonial bonds with women on earth!
And those Greek mythologists gave Zeus the sovereign power over the universe,
The right to make peace and war!
The right to sadden the humans, or to make them happy!
They also gave Zeus a wife, who would have mothered his Olympian children,
Handsome males and beautiful females known for their talents!
In one word, they gave Zeus
A family circle full of wonderful- gifted- divine beings!
Those poets also gave Zeus an immoral reputation and a promiscuous love.

---

[76] *Genesis* 6:1, 2.
[77] In *"Iliad"* and *"Odyssey"*.
[78] In *"Theogony"*.

In fact, they showed the Olympian-supreme god cheating on his wife repeatedly and in relationship with many amours and mistresses!

The Bible speaks otherwise of the true God[79]
Whose personality has nothing to do with a fairy tale!
It shows the true God giving us instruction for the sake of us!
In the Holy Scriptures, God proves to be in all circumstances a good father;
He is infinitely good and right!
He hates the evil!
He wants justice to be on earth like in the Heaven!
He blesses the righteous and punishes the wicked one.

"But knowing the true God in light of the myths
Is like seeing Him in wrath against the innocent ones too!
It is likely seeing Him punishing the righteous one and the unjust one together.
Happily, the true God does not execute his judgment that way!

By contrast, in the *Odyssey,* once Apollo[80] avenging his prophet
Would kill innocent and guilty ones without exemption!
He would perpetrate a massacre even against those begging his pardon[81]!

No innocent one ever faces a punishment on the part of the true God,[82]
The Sovereign Judge of all the Earth!
Still his severe-punitive actions target unrepentant hearts only!
And when serving the unregretful sinners with a severe sentence,
God would hate casting them to a literal-everlasting flame!

---

[79] His name is Jehovah.

[80] The ancient Greeks had also worshipped Apollo among their multiple gods. Thus, it is clear that the Greek and Latin authors have told a lot of stories about that deity.

[81] In *"The Iliad"*, namely in Book I, angry Apollo would have done blind destruction and would have killed even the animals.

[82] In the *"Genesis"*, the patriarch Abraham acknowledged that it is far from the true God to punish the innocent one with the guilty one. See Gen18:25.

He would abhor as well watching their atoning with weeping and gnashing of teeth

In an eternal-burning fire for their carnal misconducts,

I mean in this alleged place of endless torments about which some believers talk! That cruel treatment would prevent the true God

From being the embodiment of love[83] which He has always claimed to be!

As for these opposing happiness and peace on earth

And keeping impenitently challenging God's supreme decisions,

They will just die and go back to the ground where they came from!

They will become lifeless and without intelligence

After they had lost their joy, their hatred, and their love in death!

That is the condition of the dead ones!

When losing their life, they get to their own end.

And they lose their deadly soul as soon as they stop breathing!

And then the deceased ones, lifeless like a rock, can do nothing!

Nor can they speak or touch anything

Nor can they eat, suffer, or think anymore[84]

Nor can they hear a noise and even a bell sound!

Thus, I am talking to any sincere believers,

Who think that after losing their beautiful life,

They will be endlessly tormented in a hellfire!

If they want to adhere to that belief, it is up to them to do so!

And if as the poet Virgil[85] had taught in his legends

Those believers think that after they pass away

They should go to live in those mythical places,

Let them beware of such a teaching!

"In fact, there is no a punishment in a dark Tartar

Nor a field Elysees for those who are gone!

Nor an after death world in which the blessed ones and the cursed ones

---

[83]   See I *John* 4:8.

[84]   In these verses, Linda abounds according to the ideas expressed in *Psalms.* 37:10, and in *Ecclesiastes* 5:9,10

[85]   The full name of this poet was Publius Virgilius Maro. He was born in October 17, 70 BC. He wrote the *"Georgics", "Aeneid"* and *the "Eclogues".*

Would be conscious!
Nor a place where the wicked-damned one intermingles with the flawless
one!

Likewise, there has never been a multi-head dog,
A Cerberus, posted at the door to the hell!
Nor a canine that would have iron teeth
In order to scare those coming to the alleged-infernal abodes!
Nor a honey cake to soothe the mythical quadruped so it can let in
Any dead or living ones coming to that place!

Believing that a dead should pay the ferryman Charon[86] a penny
For crossing the Acheron river and getting to the after-death place,
And believing also that infernal dwelling is so putrid
That no bird can hover over it and stay alive,
All that was the product of the imagination!
It is nothing but a lie[87] which the early fabulists,
Considered like wise men passed down to the posterity,
A lie that has influenced some religions today!
For actually, many people wrongly believe that everyone has an immortal
soul[88]
Supposedly to undergo an after-death sentence in burning hell
For any unpardonable actions!
How can a dead be suffering if he is unconscious?

---

[86] According to Greek mythology, Charon would be the ferryman, or the sailor of
the underworld.
[87] Homer in the *"Iliad"* and the *"Odyssey"*, Virgil in the *"Aeneid"*, Dante in the
"Divine Comedy" have devised their own way a descent into the hell.
[88] The Bible teaches that the soul is mortal. See (*Ezekiel* 18: 4).

CHAPTER TWENTY-EIGHT

Heading for Alexandria

They had been back on board for days,
And each single couple relished an invincible love.
The cabins only could bear witnesses
Of their happiness to come there from so far!
This was time for all to indulge themselves in jubilation
As part of the cruise
Given that some of them, at the peak of their administrative career,
Just got retired!
As others, cheering in the vessel,
Delighted in touring the world with their wives
To whom they had reiterated thousand times that promise!

As others, being real singles,
Had longed for counting this journey like a souvenir,
Or had looked forward to exploring these continents
Like the husband[89] of Penelope!
Or had earnestly expected to trample the Atlantic coast
And see Africa one day before they die!

As others were found to be learned researchers, politicians, simple observers,
Students, teachers, and curious travelers,
Who wanted to see with their own eyes what they had just learned in the books,
I mean the books to which usually we resort
In case we can't afford the fare to other countries
And widen out through a trip!
And get an authentic idea of the world
And acquaint ourselves with the lifestyle of other nations living on the globe,

---

[89]   This is Ulysses the King of Ithaca, who according to that myth would be gone for a very long journey.

And get an insight into their customs and their aspirations
Into their strengths and weaknesses,
Into their xenophile manners, their ethnocentrism, and their xenophobia!

And finally remember that in the World
All people, should they be different in all respects,
They share one common thing: All they are living on Earth!
All they have inherited the same planet, this inhabited Earth,
This so perfect work of our loving Creator, Jehovah God!
The true God, the Author of any places to which we go!
This One who is entitled to our gratitude
The originator of all good things without which life would be miserable!

CHAPTER TWENTY- NINE

O Alexandria!

They had just left Crete Island, which vanished behind them from afar.
Then pining over Alexandria for which the *Adriatic Dawn* set sail,
They ran their long chats on that city.
In the meantime, Linda felt amazed at the universal interest
That everyone displayed in it.
Once again, she tried to externalize her emotions.
Therefore, she asked these questions about that Egyptian destination:

"Are there any good reasons for Alexandria to be the focus of all conversation?
How come that city has been so special this month?
Does that have to do with its recent resurrection by the archaeologists?"

"It is quite normal," answered Alberto, "to seek in the Alexandria's rebirth
The reason for it to hit the headlines!
In fact, a few cities have made the same experience as Alexandria!
We know about some of fallen metropolis which never came back.
Whether they went astray by decision of God horrified by their transgressions,
Like Sodom, Gomorrah, Babylon, Edom and so on,
Or whether they disappeared in the aftermath of a natural disaster
Like Pompey, whose inhabitants perished like in an oven!
They are never back on their feet!

By contrast, with considering Alexandria alive again with its magnificence,
I mean with its bursting lighthouse which is still guiding the Mediterranean
Like in the Ptolemaic[90] days!
With its library attracting everyone like once ago
Before it plunged into the waves,

---

[90]   After Alexander the Great died in 323 BC, a dynasty of sixteen Ptolemaic leaders
ruled over Egypt for centuries.

Everyone will attribute that focus on Alexandria to its exceptional renaissance."

"As for me," Andrea said, "I think other reasons should
Explain the unanimous interest which the passengers show in that city
As long as going away from the Greek islands they draw close to Egypt:
Alexandria reminds them of the famous warrior Alexander the Great
Whom they would like to see back from his sepulchral night!
Probably, if they could meet again that king gone long ago,
They would ask him for sure what make the difference
Between the multi-centennial constructions which he made in the city
And the new ones!
Likewise, they would ask all the Ptolemaic leaders a good question
About the previous lighthouse which forced the admiration as a global wonder!
They would like to ask those Egyptian leaders
Whether or not the new- Alexandrian tower is brighter than the former one
Formerly indispensable for the navigators coming from everywhere
Whereas Alexandria proved to be both the rotating plate of maritime trades
And the most attractive among the imperial markets inherited from Alexander."

"However, all these discussions would be pointless," Joshua said,
"If we made little account of the great minds
Who long ago lured people into Alexandria!
In fact, can we forget about the instrumental role which Archimedes and Euclid
Formerly played in the elaboration of the Alexandrian library?
Can we underestimate their contributions to that institution having welcomed all?
I mean having welcomed both the citizens and the foreigners to its enclosure?
As for me today, I would like to interrogate
Those two pioneers of the arithmetic sciences,
Who had excitingly etched their names in Alexandria!

Today, I would like to tell them face to face
How their theories have taken place
Among many others having helped the human kind
To pave its way across the civilization and get better everywhere,
I mean, everywhere technology successfully calls on science to save life
Whenever it takes efforts to rescue patients from the shackles of pests!
Whenever they should by a scientific breakthrough
Drive out the invasions of pandemics,
Which have been defeated like a hostile army
To such a point that some deadly illnesses cause less harm than before
And stop being as life threatening
As when we might die of Spanish flu, of tuberculosis, and of smallpox
And might pass away unaware of the cause of our death,
Or powerless before it while awaiting our own turn to go
If Science by a fine day comes up with nothing!

I wish I could tell Euclid and Archimedes about these death cases
Which the world was weary of, formerly!
I wish I could tell them how many were gone away tragically
Either in their hospital beds or on their operating tables!
I wish I could tell them too
How, today, many more patients of all ages leave hospitals safe and sound
After a painless treatment which spares their bemoaning and shedding tears,
Which I think is different than when death was around the corner!"

"O Gentlemen," Linda said, "I would certainly require more than one day
To talk with Archimedes and with Euclid,
About the contributions which since the time of the Ptolemy
They had brought to the current discoveries for the benefit the all nations!
Should I talk about agriculture, namely about what can be called
An arsenal of sophisticated tools and tillage equipments,
Should I choose to debate on certain grounds
Which the modern science has made so fertile
That too many supplies abound and rot in the cities,
I would speak to them so long!

I would also tell them, 'Here is what we have done!
Here are the inventions which have quite taken our beautiful world
To the peak of its glory:
We already visited other planets and came back home safe and secure!
We have transformed the world into a minuscule village
Thanks to the advanced technology of our age!
We can proudly surf the Internet and search for anything quietly!
We can perfectly see and admire anything we want,
We can from Brazil see somebody chairing a greenhouse summit in England!
From Chantal see a good soccer game occurring in Australia, or in Mongolia!

I would also cite researchers whom science holds in high esteem!
I would cite Lavoisier, Isaac Newton
Albert Einstein, Laplace, Thomas Edison
Leonard de Vinci, Kekulé, Bertholet,
The names of the scientific who invented the Internet,
Some inventors like Steve Jobs, Newman, and Bell,
John L Baird, Clement Adler, Flemming, Alfred Nobel
Samuel Colt, Samuel Morse, Joseph Montgolfier.
I would not forget about Louis Braille and Ferdinand Carré'".

"As for me," Andrea said, "I would seize the opportunity
To expose the problems which our generation has faced
Wherever science, however, makes its intervention!
I would like to ask Archimedes and Euclid if we should fully rely on technology
When considering the woes through which our world has been going
Including the daunting spectacles of devastation following natural disasters,
Like frequent earthquakes, tornadoes, and floods!
When pondering over many cases of murders and terrorist attacks
Which spare no one, not even students and teachers at school!
When considering the existence of mass destruction weapons!
When witnessing the increasing level of poverty in the Third world
And the skyrocketing joblessness rate which does more homeless
And more beggars to spend their night on sidewalk or close to trash piles!

When deploring the escalation of divorce cases everywhere
And the pains resulting from social prejudice and from racism,
When we consider the fact that many skilled people are miserable
And that in spite of their qualification they can't get a good job
As they continue lining up with their diplomas in many offices!
I would also say that nowadays literary art feeds only a few people
And that science, despite its incontestable utility, has failed like philosophy,
To provide the politicians with the ideal solution, which they have sought!
For whether they attended class in Europe, or in Alexandria,
The leaders still miss the political strategy toward the success on earth,
Despite high cost tuitions which takes years to be paid.
I would tell Archimedes and Euclid as well
No cure has been found for our woes regardless of the finest speeches
And the most pious wishes and the hugest efforts of sincere leaders!
For people keep spending their time hoping for a change that never comes!
And the happiness that they keep promising year after year remains a
dream
While the situation gets worse everywhere, which irrefutably proves
That only the Bible is right!
And I would let them know that in our situation,
The Kingdom of God is our unique hope
And the unique governmental entity capable of solving the problem of all
And providing all with a beautiful life soon!
And that it is time to advertize that Kingdom and to pray for it
Because, today, it has already appeased so many hopeless ones,
Whether they live in a castle or sleep on the street!

CHAPTER THIRTY

So Intervened Christina

"O Journeyers, could you listen to me, please?" Christine asked.
"Excuse, I beg you, the matter of my speech.
Many people, before me, dealing with astronomy
Found out how Alexandria had got involved in that discipline.
However, as they brought that science to the pinnacle,
They could not keep that city from evoking
The obstacles which the researchers encountered in their journey to the truth!
Nor could they prevent it
From recalling their mistakes in the presence of God!

Do you remember how Alexandria got stuck into Aristotle's spatial theory?
That conception took centuries to become obsolete.
The famous -Greek philosopher had located earth at the center of the universe.
And unfortunately, his thesis had made its way and misled so many people!
During many centuries, considering Aristotle as an infallible guide,
Many followers blindly adhered to his geocentricism.
In fact, the philosopher astronomer had taught about an immobile earth
That was surrounded by other planets, including the sun;
He had taught about an unsuspended earth in the void.
Unfortunately, people devoted a visceral attachment to that theory
And rejected any opposite conception!
Hence, geocentricism made its way like an absolute truth.

Other famous thinkers believed in such a system too.
Maybe had the disciple of Aristotle, Alexander the Great himself,
The founder of that city endorsed it as well without hesitation.
In this hypothesis, we can understand why from its very genesis
The Alexandrian city gave an indescribable credit to the geocentricism
And why that teaching attracted so many people!
Among the supporters of geocentricism,
There were some noteworthy researchers.

Thus, long after came Claude Ptolemy[91], a disciple of Aristotle.
Hence once again, all efforts availed little to challenge that teaching
Which became so widespread and was so blended with the truth
That it ended up in conquering the Christendom.

In the Middle-Ages, fascinated with the Greek philosophy,
Thomas Aquinas, a priest and doctor of the Church,
Commingled the Aristotelian ethics with the Catholicism!
Therefore, since the Church's authority was indisputable in many respects
And that she had the control over education,
Geocentricism was taught as an official theory.
And yet was it an aberration, it was so jealously defended
That no one could express an anti- geocentric view and remain safe!
Consequently, the physicist Galileo Galilei will later put himself in jeopardy
For exposing the falsity of the geocentric theory
And for demonstrating the truthfulness of the heliocentric conception,
Meaning, that the sun is the center of the universe!

Galileo, however, did not get the scoop on the heliocentric theory.
Centuries before, his predecessor, the Greek Aristarchus
Having explored the universe from the Alexandrian land concluded
That sun is in the middle of the cosmos!
But his heliocentric view regarded as pointless was put under fire,
Unfortunately, for the benefit of the geocentricism!
But centuries later, Nicolas Copernicus had come with the heliocentric theory too.
But he had failed as well, for the Church was geocentric.

Now we can understand
That Church should turn Galileo down with his heliocentric views.
The Catholic Inquisition will even compel him to deny his theory.
However, his system was the one reflecting the word of the Creator.
In fact, Galileo thought that earth hangs like a moving circle in the space!

---

[91]   The Ptolemaic science was named after the astronomer Claude Ptolemy, not after
the leaders of the Ptolemaic dynasty. According to researchers, it is unlikely that
the learned Claude Ptolemy has had family ties with the members of the royal
family of the Ptolemy.

And that's exactly what the Bible[92] had said long ago before that serious conflict.
Facing the Inquisition in those circumstances,
Galileo had a narrow escape from danger!

He ran the risk of passing for a rebellious
And of expiring in the pitiless flame which charred the bodies of the heretic
At the time of the infamous martyrdoms inflicted in the name of God
Even for things which were known to be true!
But today it turns out that technology has ended that deception
And has brought the speeches to their conclusion
By saying who was wrong, who was right!
To sum up, all these conflicts must remind us
That despite their knowledge, men are limited
And that they need help, look, I mean, the true help of God
So they can discover the truth about which they are often speculating!

---

[92]   See Job 26:7, Isaiah 40:22

CHAPTER THIRTY-ONE

So Talked Christina's Husband

"O pleasant listeners, could you hear my laments?
I am talking about an issue which bugs me!" Christian said, at last.
"What I am exposing to you today sickens me whenever I ponder over it:

Once ago, many know about it, numerous were expatriated Jews in Alexandria.
In fact, with time elapsing, these descendants of Abraham
Became more fluent in the Hellenic language than in Hebrew!
Therefore, they wanted the Moses Law given their ancestors
To be translated into Greek.
To make their dream come true,
They obtained from the Alexandrian leaders the permission
To invite seventy experts on Moses Law to their Egyptian-new homeland!
Consequently, under the aegis of the Alexandrian king[93],
The Septuagint[94], the first Greek version of the Bible, was achieved.
That undertaking was expected to fill the spiritual needs of that Jews community.
It would serve the interest of the non-Jews as well!
Many non-Israelites, in fact, were attracted by the lifestyle of the Israel nation,
By its institutions, its cult, and its altar!
Many non- Israelites were intrigued to know
About the significance of the Holy Covenant[95]
That created a particular link between the true God and that nation.

---

[93]   Ptolemy Philadelphus, so called for marrying his sister Arsinoe.
[94]   The first Greek translation of the Hebrew Scriptures
[95]   According to Exodus 24: 3-8, all the sons of Israel were involved in bilateral covenant with Jehovah, which had made them a saint nation and a chosen race.

Politically, such an undertaking would provide the Alexandrian leaders
With all the social and religious information which they needed
To make the best decisions for their Alexandrian-Jews subjects!
As known everywhere on earth,
While living abroad, those Jews would remember
That Jehovah, their master and their savior,
Had spoken to their ancestors on the Sinai Mount
And that they should stay away from the pagan practices
Which were in vogue in the Alexandrian land!

Though there is no need to say what role the *Septuagint* would play
In the life of these Alexandrian Jews
Who felt the need to invoke the true God from whom they felt far
And to talk to Him as their Holy Father
Who could anytime hear their sincere prayers
Whenever they would call His name and distinguish Him from the false
gods.
Alas, Friends, today, I deplore the fact that
The name of the true God has fled from the *Septuagint!*
Who is at fault? And for what have they removed His name from that
translation?

Is not Jehovah worthy of our love anymore as in that time,
I mean when the Jews invoked His name?
Who can deny Him the right to be different than all the thousands false
gods?
Is not He our Friend and Confidant anymore, He who knows us better
than all?
He who showed His name so we can call Him through severe trials!
Why have we tried to make Him an anonymous God while we all have
a name?
Is not that a kind of disdain towards Him?

Since we have removed His name from the Bible,
We have been exposed to many more woes!
For forgetting about our heavenly Father,
Some people exasperate Him much more by their misconducts!
They have lost their fear of the Supreme Judge
Whose Judgment remains, however, the same!
They have forgotten that they are accountable for their misdeeds
When comes the day[96] for Him to judge the whole-entire Earth
And to remind the wicked ones that
He, Jehovah, created the universe and that He is always the same!"

Finally, the travelers landed in the wonderful-Alexandrian city
That had been thought to be buried forever.
At the first rays of the sun, they landed in this Alexandria, recently rebuilt.
Then they got ready to explore the land.
And the visiting crowd swarmed the city,
Especially to discover the traces of the past,
And to enlighten themselves behind the guides on what had been once ago
Both the land of the Ptolemy and other prestigious-Egyptian cities,
No matter whether they are called Memphis, or Heliopolis!

---

[96] This day in question is the Battle of Armageddon which fortunately is coming
soon.

CHAPTER THIRTY-TWO

On the Nile River

For the first time on the Nile River, Linda saw that water,
That majestic water which had witnessed the passage of so many kings!
Now on the Nile, formerly changed into blood,
She thought of the ten plagues having caused the exodus of an abused
nation!
Then going to Luxor to the tombs of the kings,
She saw of the Pharaohs the ancient necropolis
Which hides its secrets behind thousands enigmatic scriptures!
Then at the foot of the pyramids
She felt her mind filled with multiple issues
About written and unwritten monuments which the guide was showing!
And through a silent soliloquy she told the vestiges,

Tell me, O Pyramids!
Had people tried sometimes to empty your multi-centennial depots?
If so, to what piece of land had they carried your stuffs?
Tell me, please, what waterways had aided in the transportation of your
goods.
Had the shippers used the Mediterranean at which your tops look?
And had the Atlantic Sea assisted the looters of your gold?
That gold which many people would have liked to exploit!

How many like us from the Caribbean have you let in your enclosure?
How many sultans, how many viziers
Have taken their families to yours realms?
How many came here, whether they were Medes, from Persians, or from
Greece
Whether they were ancient Romans or Chaldean,
How many came here?
How many conquerors and despots have left their footprints in your
premises?
How many came to Luxor to see your charms and your decrepit caves?

Since the austere- hieroglyphic alphabet challenged Napoleon
And that Champollion[97] unveiled its mystery, have you resented the latter?
Have you resented the temple of Karnak and its stone gods which
Allowed foreign hands to sack you?
Yet could not the researchers elucidate all your mysteries
Which thousands years have concealed in the tombs;
Yet could no one do it
Even at the light of the military torches!"

Soon after, they left for Memphis to see other pyramids
By that beautiful day,
They rode their camels to Memphis across arid valleys and hills.

---

[97]   Jean-François Champollion was the first to decipher the hieroglyphics of Egypt.

CHAPTER THIRTY-THREE

Goshen

Linda and her five fellows arrived to Goshen where
They listened carefully to their friendly cicerone talking about the City.
"It was here," the guide Absalom said,
"That Joseph had established his brothers, the sons of Israel.
At that time, the pharaoh invited those immigrants
To enjoy the best food of the country;
However centuries later, contemplating their countless population
A new Pharaoh decided on enslaving them!
He subdued all those descendants of Abraham
To the fabrication of bricks in a very tough condition!
Moreover, the heartless king resorted to a deadly strategy
To stop their population from growing up by killing the new- born males!
For the new Egyptian ruler wrongly considered
That the presence of so many Israelites could be a threat for the Egyptians!
In the meantime, tired of all those infamous sacrileges and barbarities,
The Hebrews implored the intervention of Jehovah, the God of their ancestors.
'Could you fly and rescue us, O God of our forefathers!
Could you free us from all our atrocities coming from our pitiless executioners?
Oh! See how they torture us from time to time!
Could you from your heavenly dwelling hear our incessant groaning!
And see our newborn sons hopelessly falling under infanticide blades!'

God taking pity on their suspiring thrived to break their yoke and their shackles.
He got so angry at the stubborn- Egyptian monarch
That He gave him an ultimate lesson:
He killed him and his army in the water of the Red Sea.
Then God magnified His name through that hecatomb!

For the God of Jacob wanted all the kings to know
That He is the strongest and the greatest sovereign!
And that He can reduce to nothing the pitiless rulers!
You all know, however, what happened later:
Those freed Israelites will quit God who had saved them.
And they will lose his compassion."

CHAPTER THIRTY-FOUR

Linda's Meditations

It was dusk. In her Egyptian hotel Linda sat down alone.
She was musing over the sons of Jacob having moved to that city long ago.
She recollected everything the guide had said about them and wondered
Why the loving God would have rejected his chosen nation.
In search for an answer, she recalled both the Jeremiah's and Isaiah's prophecies.
And she tried to answer the previous question in a soliloquy
That looked like a prayer to God.

"O God!" Linda exclaimed. "How often you spoke to them!
But this rebellious nation trivialized your holy words
And forgot, alas, about their past!
They stepped on your covenant which should end all woes at an appointed day!
In your infinite and sublime love,
You kept your legitimate wrath from exploding against them!
Yet did they persist in their strong disobedience,
You continued exhorting them by means of your prophets!
You told them about all the gravity of their sins
And forewarned them against the punitive attacks
To shortly come from the pagan nations!
And you even promised to forgive them
If they really felt sorry for their transgressions!

But despite your great love, this obdurate nation
Kept doing whatever could make you mad at them,
Young, old, males, and females,
Who all led before you a carnal existence!
Whatever you abhor, O most Sovereign God,
It was what they practiced in your Holy presence!
In their fornication which you had in disgust
They saw a permanent and delightful hobby!

To the false gods they kept offering their children
By invoking so impure idols before you!
Although they all knew that you are jealous, O God,
They kept upsetting you with all their sacred posts!
And that way, they copied the neighboring nations
So much so that one day, fed up with their badness
You wanted to move them from the face of their land
And sent the Chaldeans to their territory!
For you choose whomever to punish your children
And have them stay away from their disobedience!

Then Nebuchadnezzar obeying your order
Encircled their country and besieged it for long!
At that view, your nation far from surrendering,
Preferred to resist your chosen Chaldean king!
Meanwhile was rampant the ruthless starvation
Causing many mothers to eat their own children!
What a barbarity, God, during that blockade!

The Judean monarch finally ran away
And got easily caught on the run to a bush!
And then he was taken to the Chaldean king
Who decided on his end and on his household's!
Under the order of the proud conqueror
The Judean king saw his sons' execution
Before he got his both eyes cruelly gouged out!
Worse yet, did the victor condemn other princes
To finish by the edge of the Chaldean sword!
Meanwhile, were burning and the homes and the camps
And the Temple despoiled of its sacred vessels!
And then you stopped, O God, you stopped intervening
You stopped choosing a king for your captive nation
Which then under the yoke of their new proud masters,
Should recall all the laws given their ancestors
All those things which they missed in their captivity
Including actually the Holy covenant

That made them so special for their Father and God
As a victorious people feared everywhere!

They envisioned that time when their great victories
Brought their defeated ones to fear you, Jehovah!
They remembered that time when your omnipotence,
Was the source of their pride, of their singular fame!
And then year after year, and then week after week,
They dreamed of the country once their own property:
All that land had become the den of the jackals,
A place of which brambles harbored all the vipers!

Oh! It is worth asking, O my God, how come
You who had fought for them all the other nations
How come you let them fall into others' hands?
But as you kept silent during their punishment,
You took pity on them and felt their suffering!
You always scotched all plans against their survival!
You even cursed all these wanting their destruction.
For although you did hate all their impious actions,
You wanted them to beget the posterity
Who should of the Serpent crush the infamous head!
Therefore, after seventy years of captivity,
O God, you freed them all from their Babylonian yoke
And brought them to their dwellings back,
So they could rebuild their country, the Temple, and their rampart.

CHAPTER THIRTY-FIVE

Good Bye, Angelo,

And the six companions were visiting Cairo
Where Joshua and Linda having left the cruise
Yearned for going to the Atlantic coast whence they would return later to
America.

Although they were tired, the couple still had a gigantic task to carry out:
They craved for exploring the Black African countries
That had played a role in their history!
They ached for landing in Benin
From which came the parents of Toussaint Louverture
They yearned for treading the Congolese land
Where their Haitian countrymen have lived for decades!
They thirsted for entering the Senegal
So they could see the route of the slavers
From the Gorée Island to anywhere in the World;
In Senegal as well they expect to learn more about [98]Bantu conquests
That hugely favored the slave trade!
They itched for going to Dakar
And discovering the traces of the attractive *"Signares"*[99]!

Then, the moment came for them to farewell their wonderful co-journeyers.
Oh! How bitter was that separation!
Especially, when Alberto with a tender and sensitive voice
Said what grief and what suffering were tearing his heart
By seeing them taking their leave!

"Today," he said, "it grieves me to realize again
That your grandmother Denise is not still alive, Joshua!

---

[98]   For some people, the Bantu represent the whole black Africa. For others, they are only a part of the black Africa.

[99]   They called "signares" a noble woman born in the in matrimonial bond between a Portuguese nobleman and a Senegalese woman.

If she were living, she would have to come here and say good bye to you too
After we spent so beautiful days in Venice, in Athens, and here in Egypt,
Enjoying ourselves with cheerful mind and drunken soul!
O my children, only God knows how much she would bewail over your departure
After we animated so many debates on board!
O Joshua, my son, O my dear Linda,
Let God facilitate you a happy egress through Addis Ababa!
And I wish you could make a joyful crossing from there to your people in Congo
And go back safely to Haiti soon!

We will never forget about our ineffable tour which had cheered us up every day.
How sad I feel for letting you go, my children!
Please, come back as soon as possible!"
Then by that lovely morning,
Joshua and his wife with tearful eyes took their leave from Cairo
Whereas there was an exchange of heartbreaking goodbyes on both sides!

CHAPTER THIRTY-SIX

Welcome to Kinshasa

Joshua bringing Linda to the Congo[100] Kinshasa
Was eager to meet there one of his parent's loyal friends, Mr. Laventure,
Who had moved to that country four decades ago!
When he was a teen,
Joshua heard his parents grieving the eternal absence of Laventure from Haiti.
He knew as well about his parents' project
To visit that old colleague in his new African homeland!
Alas! He saw their passing away before they could concretize that dream!
That's why, now in remembrance of them,
He decided on spending some days with their old friend in Kinshasa.

Mr. Laventure went to that country as a talented teacher
To assist the Congolese youth right after the independence of Congo.
Since then, he stayed there permanently as many compatriots
Who never think about quitting that country that has conquered their love!

For the present, Laventure is getting old over there.
And he still has no plan to undertake the journey to his Haitian motherland
Where, living as a single, he had left family, friends, and properties,
Which he might wistfully remember sometimes!
Therefore, we can anticipate his excitement
While waiting for his two visitors in Kinshasa.
In that morning, he stayed at the entrance to welcome the couple Trazileon.
Once that he saw them, so he poured his wonderment out:

"Is that really you, Joshua? Oh! How you take after your father!
Blessed be the heaven who led your steps to my humble abode in Kinshasa today!
I'm ready now! Yes, I can go my way!

---

[100]   The Belgian Congo won independence June 30, 1960

I can go to my last dwelling with peace and serenity!
In fact, seeing you concretizes all my dream,
A dream which remained the same whether I slept or woke up:
Oh! How I wished I could talk to you face to face someday
Before expiring under the weight of my years!

"O beloved son, I still recollect the ambiance
In which I witnessed your birth in Turgeau!
About fifty years had elapsed since you threw your all first smile at me!
At that time, I was next to your kind father
A good friend as much as a sincere confidant!
No need to say how happy I was to rock you in my arms
As long as you were uttering your wailings!
For as a spoiled child, you cried loudly, which worried your mother a lot!
Today, I am seeing her again singing her sweet lullabies to calm you down!
For your defunct mother with her so tender voice
Experienced a great joy singing them all to you
Up to the time when, you, conquered by sleep,
You came to a standstill until the next day!
O my God, I recall everything as if it just took place yesterday!
So I feel so proud to welcome you to Congo today
And share this wonderful souvenir with you!

Sincerely, I would never think that far from my native land
Would be mine that unrivaled pleasure, this morning!
Welcome to you Joshua! Welcome to your wife as well!
That singular beauty, so worthy of your flame!
My wife, my son, and my grandsons,
All of them will be fully happy to make your acquaintance!
In fact, once that they heard about your visit,
They were looking forward to seeing who you are
For, I spent so much time talking about you as my loving son!"

At these words, our couple was brought to tears.
They were so amazed at this very warm welcome!
Then Joshua at the peak of his emotion,
Thus responded in turn to show his own affection to the old friend:

"Oh! How touched I am, Mr. Laventure!
By your loving words which assure me that you really are
The exceptional heart whom my parents talked about
When they told me they had in this country
Their most sincere and their dearest friend,
A rare brother whom they love as their own flesh!
When they told me how sad they had felt
To see you one day taking your luggage and leaving for this unknown country,
Even if it were for few years or for a short-term contract!
And when they said that since you had left them, you have forgotten the way back
And have made them waited for you on a daily basis
Until the wicked death took them!

What a pity! They are gone!
After they vainly caressed their beautiful dream
Of coming here and embracing you!
And reminding you that they still loved you!
For your name repeated so loudly in their conversation
Even if, nowadays, has died simply the true love!
Therefore tell me, please, in what circumstances
You have kept this eloquent silence to your natal land!
Tell me what bad remembrance of it has prevented you from treading it again!
Was your life put in jeopardy to such point that
You felt compelled to take the road to exile?
Who is that offended you in such way
That you punished us with an eternal absence?
Or could it be that an imposing force sticks you to the Congolese land
And bans you from retreading your Haitian motherland
And hearing the songs of our nightingales
And seeing our avian legions raiding our rice fields
And admiring the convoy of our butterflies
As the autumn sun greets forests and clearings
And confiding your hobbies to the great care of our beaches

Where everybody feels attracted to the endless immersions into the water
Whereas at the shore,
Vagrant musicians providing the gift of their charming voice,
Endlessly, orchestrate their love, their sufferings,
Their passion, their joy of troubadours,
Endlessly, sing out their dreams, their happiness, and their erotic conquests
Which, together, creates an aura of happiness?

Perhaps will you argue that the African land offers you the same rustic charm!
And that the beautiful sun invites all to enjoy themselves everywhere
I mean, in any places where it rises!
In fact, we must lie, if we claim to close the door of our heart
To the souvenir coming from the enchanting land on which we were born!
For no matter how old we are,
We often feel homesickness overcome our hearts!"

"O beloved son," Laventure replied,
"I feel your words as sweet as hard!
For, my conscience accuses me of a crime which is worth your legitimate ire.
I feel hit and crushed with a sword, my son!
I don't know why I have betrayed both your father and your mother,
The only friends who were on earth in solidarity with me and with my cause!
Yes! I asked myself that question sometimes!

In fact, I continue loving my natal country
Even if far away from it I have stayed to serve other peoples for so long!
Indeed, what do I have to blame on the good Haitian land?
It taught me how to love my own people!
And how to help a lot of nations get out of their sufferings and their tribulations!
It shows me how to enjoy the pleasures which freedom offers!
How to stay away from servile chains and cruelty!
It shows me how to treat the foreigner properly!
How to love him and serve him with joy and goodness

To such a point that, sometimes, all our compatriots think
That we prefer the foreigners than them!

To tell the truth, while the outsiders enjoy our lands,
One could doubt that our Haitian brothers take advantage of them!
Yes while others coming from abroad flock to our treasures,
Ourselves we remain nostalgic outside, missing forever our sunbath!
Suffering from anxiety and sleeplessness!
Troubled by our alarms and sleeping on the train
To be on time at their workplaces!
Thank God! I was not cornered into exile
When I arrived here by an April morning to educate the Congolese youth!
Nor did I intend to stay here all that time or to be here forever!
Even if I agree with you that I should give up my indifference
And visit my own country after such a long absence!
Yes! I intend to go there, against winds and tides!
Then, I will feel my conscience soothed."

"Wherever we live,
We should find it wise to visit your own people." Linda said.
"And it will help a lot to do so.
No matter whether we live among the Persians, or the Medes,
Or acquire a new name or new nationality in another country,
We should not feel bad about treading our motherland again!
Since the whole entire earth belongs to our Great Creator, Jehovah!"

CHAPTER THIRTY-SEVEN

A Trip with Mr. Laventure

It was in the Kinshasa that the couple spent their most beautiful days!
They were so happy that they got relief from their fatigue.
In fact, they felt treated like two pashas by Laventure.
Their old host walked them also through the attractions of the city
And accompanied them through Brazzaville,
The birthplace of the girl who once had conquered his love!
Unhappily, the gleeful visitors had to leave shortly.
And today they still remember those locations
That reminded them of their own Haitian country:
Lubumshashi, whose green flowerbed they left against their will!
Mbandaka, which seduced Linda
To such a degree that she would like to build a castle on its shore
And enjoy herself in it for the rest of her life!
Matadi, whose coconut trees and population made them feel in their own land
Mostly when the sunlight blazes!
And Bukavu[101], whose beauty conquered their love
So they would like to come back to its sites in the future!

---

[101] Bukavu Lumbushashi, Matadi M- badaka are Congolese cities.

CHAPTER THIRTY-EIGHT

The Last Outing

At their final excursion, Laventure escorted his guests to the Congo River.
And on the edge of that waterway,
He told them how sick he had felt after leaving his country!
And how he had dreamed about Port-au-Prince at every single night!
He also told them how had missed the sun rising over the Morne Hôpital.[102]

On the verge of this waterbed,
He let them know how he had longed for that past!
And how his homesickness inspired him multiple lines
That had attenuated his profound melancholy!

At the brink of this river flow,
He told them how his melodious rhymes
Had gained him the love of Macumba,
The attractive Congolese whose presence in his life has enlivened him!

Pretty near the Congo River,
The visiting couple lost their hearts to Laventure's romantic poems
Of which *"Sugar Cane"* was their favorite one.
"Would you mind declaiming that poetry for us?" They asked Laventure
Who was so glad to do it as follows:

"O Sugar Cane, please, tell about your story!
Tell all without exception, tell the lovers of the good wine
Tell them, I beg you, what glory was yours not long ago!
Doing so for now, keep silent, please,
In behalf of the profligates whom your drink intoxicates!
Silence, please, on those enjoying alcohol to distraction
As they vainly seek consolation in it!
In this account, please, say how many have failed
To find true happiness in the Dionysian nights

---

[102]   That mountain is situated in Port-au-Prince.

Where love, apoplectic with rage,
Invites you to assist his enchanting exploits!
Keep silent, please, on the Epicureans
Who want to pass away with their bottles in hand!
As they think that abusing alcohol will bring them
An ultimate pleasure on earth before they die!
Please, forget about these endless sybarites
Who explore in drunkenness an unlimited joy!
Forget the hedonists seeking in cathouse an insidious pleasure!
Silence in your story, Cane, about these homes
In which people get drunk to such a way that one day
The Law separates Joseph from Marianne!
That husband indulging in alcoholism
Drank all his salaries and came home so bitter
That he treated all his own people like enemies!

But, Cane, while telling about your history,
Could you remind us why throughout your career
You chose your associates among so cruel people
Who have soiled your glory and tarnished your good fame?
God had created you to gladden humans' heart,
Not to see you causing so horrifying crimes
By which men used to treat their neighbors like real beasts!
O Cane, once, however, you had the greedy ones
Subdue ebony skins to your exploitation
Without salaries! under whips and sorrows!
Oh! How many ships did not you see on sea!
Set sail morning and night to the Goree[103] Island?
How many did you bring from Nantes or Bordeaux[104]
To the reified and desperate-human cargos?

---

[103] This island is located near Dakar, Senegal. From there in part the slaves were shipped to America.

[104] According to historians, the slavers departed from Bordeaux, Nantes, La Rochelle, and Saint-Malo.

O Cane, didn't you see many rivers of tears
That endlessly flowed from desperate faces?
From the eyes of those who forever left their land
For wherever might lead their slavish existence
After they had lost all: freedom, happiness, love?
O Cane, how many did you see at that time
Sold, shackled, powerless, and crammed into wedges?
All these souls bewailing over their families
Whom all they had then lost, I mean, lost forever?

How many expired after long starvation
Or died in the wedges of cruel suffocation?
O Sugar Cane, that way you saw many perish
And feed the sea across their sad misadventures!
And the seamen you saw, look, the heartless seamen
Who took trouble seeing the loss of human goods!
You saw them who then coerced the survivors to sing
For fear that their sadness might destroy all of them!

After their long journey, finally here's the land
Which you took to the peak of its prosperity
At the cost of their dark and austere existence!
Saint-Domingue[105], where many of them had been sold!
Where their buyers took them in leash to their fields!
Where all their suffering under servile labors
Inspired them of life and disgust and hatred!
Then, under the cruel yoke of sadistic masters,
Who whipped them until blood for a peccadillo!
They needed to be strong and be strong like a mule
To receive more whippings than their own nourishment![106]

---

[105] Of course, they were marketed in all the colonies. But slavery was more inhumane in the colony of Saint- Domingue than elsewhere.

[106] See *Les Jacobin Noirs* By Historian James.

It was there that, O Cane, against the human kind
You caused new abuses to come to existence!
When the usual tortures seemed not to be enough
To compel all the slaves to provide windfalls!
May-be did they borrow from the Inquisition[107] its inhumane torture!
O Cane, remember it!
For Church[108] saw no badness[109] in those atrocities!
Therefore, tell me, O Cane, tell me who was at fault
Whenever slaves were cast to boiling molasses?
Or when Monster Caradeux[110] delighted in their woes?
Tell me who was at fault when of the servile flock
Some got sometimes roasted in the furnaces bread?[111]
Tell me who was at fault when executioners
Seeing them, not like men, killed them like animals!
Tell me who was at fault when tired of their throe
Many of them chose then to expire serenely?
Cane, whose fault if the whip of the cruel commanders
Deeply cut their dark skin! While set face down and tied up on four pegs
They screamed and sighed hopelessly?

All of them are guilty before the history,
I mean all who grew you in search for sordid gain!
For their prosperity at the cost of men's life!
They are guilty, all those who mistakenly thought
That they should build their joy, their happiness as well
On the weaker ones' woe by killing their freedom!

---

[107] In fact, the methods of torture used against the slaves in the colony were not more inhumane than those of the Inquisition.

[108] Article 2 of the 1685 Black Code stipulated that slaves were to be maintained in the discipline of the Roman Catholic Church. So there is no doubt that the slaves of Saint -Domingue practiced the same religion as their masters.

[109] To tell the truth, in Saint- Domingue, Catholic missionaries such as the Capuchins and the Jesuits used to show a certain compassion for the slaves. However, the Vatican did not condemn the slave trade and the servile tortures

[110] Caradeux is presented by the historians as one of the most sadistic masters in Saint-Domingue.

[111] The cruelty of the Colonists was limitless in Saint- Domingue.

They are guilty all those who had blessed the Slave Trade
By giving their consent to all the traffickers!
All those who, once ago, preached love on the pulpit
And made their own fortune by using the system!
Cane, if once ago Europe delighted in you
How bitter you tasted in the Africa's mouth!
Look how her children should pass away for you
In their sad condition once in America!

O Cane, it's coming soon the so nice day for you
To taste well sweet in all people's palate on earth!
Then all races will have to realize forever
That regardless of our epidermal nuances,
We are bound on earth to love ones another!
For the Kingdom of God will destroy slavery soon
As well as its sequel so none will remember it!
Then God will establish his millenary reign
At which many defunct slaves will come back to life!"
The visiting couple exclaimed then exclaiming 'bravo!'

CHAPTER THIRTY-NINE

On the Way Back to Home

Finally, the couple said good bye to Mr. Laventure.
Then there were sadness and tears in all faces.
After so many good surprises
Joshua and Linda would be back to their country so soon!
Since dawn, on their flight to New York,
As they monitored any little chocks on the aircraft,
They were eager to return to the bosom of their family.
By the time, Linda getting tired of the long journey fell asleep.
But as for the husband, he killed time composing these lines:

"In the chariot of my poetry,
I tear the space and the time by flying to get fun
Like the butterfly sporting in the fields!
I cross the line of the human nature as my soul mulls over
All having lived only the space of a morning,
All lying today in the nothingness!
All those to come back soon by divine decision,
Whether they had lived on earth as lords or as rascals!
Whether they had seen their end on board the Titanic
Or in Roman forum at griffons' hungry jaws!
Or ended on scaffolds for defending their faith!
Whether they died in sea or in the catacombs!
Whether they qualified at their death for a tomb
Unlike those whom God cursed as remorseless sinners!
I let my soul mull over all of them.

On the wings of my lines I fly across the time
And I ask the history
About those dying without their glory!
About those having left as they came out of their mother
Without any wealth and gold and diamond
While coming naked for an ephemeral time!

On the wings of my lines
I ask about those whom the greatest silence
Releases from their ordeals
After they lived on earth through many tears and sighs
And went across so much humiliation!
As did once the Sudras deemed as untouchable!
As did all those found to be declared unclean
Due to their leprosy, their smallpox and other plagues then out of control.
As did those to be born to be slaves in the earlier time!

In the chariot of my verses,
I grieve the ignorance of all those who got buried at their king's funeral
So they could continue serving the dead monarchs
During their allegedly after death existence!
I grieve the condition of all little sold boys
Who being castrated should sing well in choirs!
I grieve all those who through their odious sufferings
Remained yet so loyal in Nazi- infamous camp of concentration!
Remained loyal despite the heinous gas chambers
Where starving and skeletal
They welcomed death and stayed loyal to the true God!

On the wings of my verses,
I fly from night to dawn and admire the ether,
I observe the heavens that Jehovah adorns with all the cosmos' lights,
This glittering army which He, the Logos' father
Brought for His saint glory to the beautiful existence
So the cheerful poet can delight in His magnificence
And come to compose a poem
And glorify His name, a name which so many senseless ones ignore!
A name which ignores only a fearless heart!
For they'd better recognizing now that Jehovah is the True God
And that He will bring back to life
All the missing ones whose death has saddened Him!"

Just after Joshua was finished writing this poem
That he fell asleep himself and lowered his head on Linda
Who whispered to him, "I love you, Honey!"

CHAPTER FORTY

Finally, Here You Are, Mom!

There was in the villa a festive atmosphere
When the jubilant couple came back
And showed many pictures and thousand souvenirs of the visited countries,
Including the photos taken on board the ship;
"Happy is he that like Odysseus did a nice trip![112]*"* Joshua exclaimed.
They particularly exulted over hugging their sons
Whom they had missed for so long!
All the more as so they found them safe and sound!

We remember how much Linda missed her two boys
So much so that she got a dream in their behalf!
She could not wait to see those children in her lap.
In the meantime, she fully forgot about Jain
As if he, that out-wedlock-first born son, did not exist!

Three days later Jain dropped by the villa.
Happily at the same time,
Joshua was dropping his two sons at school!
As for the maid Marianne, she had gone to Babiole[113]
To see her father suffering from typhoid!

With an optimistic and well innocent look
Then Jain arrived to his mother's splendid house.
And he expected to be warmly welcomed by her
And to see his endless sadness end right away!
But upon seeing him,
Linda panicked and started to lash out at him
And suddenly she calmed down and said something
That brought hope and brightness to the Jain's existence.

---

[112] Joshua had learned these verses from the poem *Les Regrets*, Sonnet XXXI by Joachim du Bellay
[113] Babiole is located not far from the villa of the Trazileon

"What a shame! I'm lost!
So early you come here, bad boy!" She yelled at him.
"Who gave you permission, Jain, to climb up to here,
And disturb this early morning my happiness?
How dare you to come here and see me?
When I spoke to you, didn't you understand me?
I told you nobody should know that you are my son!
Don't you remember that at the funeral of my mom
I told everybody you are my little cousin!
For Joshua, my husband, would drive me crazy
If he discovered that I am your real mother!
He would not take it lightly at all!

I would owe him a clear explanation about you!
And I even believe that Joshua would hang me,
If he knew about that! For sure, he would hate me!
As for my two children and the Trazileo,
I think they would be furious against me as well!
All my people would cast me, Jain, to a lion's den!
Not only would I have to lose their good esteem,
I would expose myself to their righteous disgust
For failing to tell them you had been eight years old
When coming to my life that good man married me!"

After saying that word,
Linda gazing at Jain's desperate- crying face
Took pity on her son,
And then she poured out her all remorse as follows:

"Oh! How brainless I am to react so badly!
O my son! Forgive me for hurting you that way!
No matter what happened,
I will remain your mom in the bottom of me!
Forgive me! I am your mom! And I love you so much!
But I managed to hide my faults to my husband
Who has loved me so much!
And he really makes me the only one woman

Who has never ever been shown a so deep love!
The only wife to be entrusted with such a wealth
That, I can't swear, has piled up near the moon, O Jain!
No, my son, I don't want to meet you here again
For fear that he might see that I am your mother
And come to detest me!
Please, get out of here, leave this house quick, Jain!
Please, take your leave from this villa immediately!
Do it please and never come back here as you did!
For if you remains here,
I will betray myself through my body language!
And they will come to know about my secret!
Go, go, stay where you are. I'll come there to see you
To perform my motherly duties toward you!
Sure, I will fill the void which you feel in your heart
And prove to be for you an affectionate mom!
And mostly on your part,
Swear me you won't let the cat out of the bag!
Beware of revealing Jain our secret affair
To anyone asking you who your mother is!
And refrain from telling him in what circumstance
That great distance once happened between you and me!"

"Wholeheartedly, I agree with you!" Jain replied.

Jain had never heard his mom speak so tenderly!
For now, no need to say how amazed he felt!

"I will do anything you want," he said, "Mother,"
I want your happiness, and not your misfortune.
And I'm going back right now to my host's house
In which I have expected to see you for a month
So that a second time in my all existence
I could hear you telling me you love me today!
And honestly, I thought you denied me for real!
I thought you denied all my begging for your love
Which I missed since the year you had brought me to life!

I'm leaving you now and I am looking forward to seeing you!
Please, come and talk to me, I thirst for hearing you!
It's really what I wish I could see in you, Mom,
That you show me that I have a place in you love!
Your love for me is worth more than this great castle
More than this luxurious and glitzy dwelling
More than all of those goods to which they sacrifice
Their happiness without finding a real life!"

Then, Linda warmly hugging Jain told him good bye.
He left the place swiftly, happy to have conquered
The affection of his mom, which he had missed for long!
He hoped he had gained her love again forever!
Since then, the mother thrived to fill his son's love need
But she wished she could tell her husband all someday.

CHAPTER FORTY-ONE

Filial Gratefulness

Six years later, Jain turning seventeen
Was as a successful-young man to many respects!
He led a happy life in Port-au-Prince and possessed his own bank account.
He planned to go to college and become an architect.
He kept secret his parentage links to Linda
Who had brought so much joy to his existence and dispelled his loneliness.

At his age, Jain became a strong man already.
He practiced some sports.
He knew very well how to use a shovel, a handsaw, a hoe and so on.
He also valued the literary art
That he thought can more likely make the delight a distinguished person.

By an evening, while waiting for Linda,
Jain wrote a sonnet to thank her for everything she had done for him.
O My Beautiful Mother is the title of that poem.

"O Mother, O my most beautiful woman,
I wish I could get of an angel the wonderful wings
And fly up to the heaven at the feet of our Father,
And tell in your favor my fervent prayer!

Fortunately, our God from the heavens listens
To those praying on earth with faith and no doubt
In the name of his son! Ah, may He hear today
All my requests for you who've been so kind to me!

May He do that one day I am useful to you
And prove to be for you an arm which you rely on!
An unalterable support in danger time!

Then you will remember, O my unique mother,
That it was worth making all your sublime effort
To bring me back to life through your maternal love!"

Just after the mother had heard these fourteen lines
That she felt so touched from the bottom of her heart
And grieved the fact that his son had missed once all first tenderness!

CHAPTER FORTY-TWO

A Happy-Worrying Mother

Linda was crazy for her son's poem.
It was a real expression of his thankfulness for her sacrifice in his favor.
While analyzing the theme of gratitude in the sonnet,
She realized that it was worth being so kind to him!
In fact, she has done everything to drive out of his heart the feeling
That he was an abandoned child and someone bound to distress on earth.
It is evident that in spite of her long absence from Jain's life,
She, finally, took the habit of spoiling him
And gave him a sincere demonstration of her motherly love
As usually she did for the sake of her legitimate sons.
As a matter of fact, when this relationship became stronger,
Linda saw in this nurtured-first -born son her most sincere confidant.
Consequently, she thought that she well deserved his prayer
By which he had asked his celestial Father for her blessing
And had promised to help and protect her.
Jain's wishes looked sincere to her
Although on her part she never expected any bad things to happen
That could ruin her happiness
And put her at the expenses of her first born and out-wedlock son.
Thence, the only one thing which she needs to be happy
Is to inform her husband that she is the mother of Jain!
She will need to do so very carefully,
For this news may upset the husband and cause him to break up with her!

CHAPTER FORTY-THREE

A Good Association

Jain lived in downtown Port-au-Prince.

He had dwelled on Macajoux Street in his own apartment for ten years.

Usually, he welcomed a lot of friends to his living-room

Where took place important debates over religious issues.

But at last, all of them agreed

That only the Bible contains the appropriate answers to many questions.

Among his friends, however,

The oldest one had particularly a positive influence on him.

Did Jain need an advice?

This 'brother', Theodore would always volunteer to mentor him.

Consequently, Jain saw in his advisor both a confidant and a father.

In turn, the latter considered him like his own son.

He helped the young man take wise decisions

And saved him from winding paths and hassle!

To sum up, Jain made a good choice in friendship matter.

He got into association with people who treated him fraternally!

Moreover, it was only after a natural disaster crushed Port-au-Prince

That Jain would know how deeply his friends loved him.

CHAPTER FORTY-FOUR

Unexpected Things Occurred

Quiet was the atmosphere.
An eloquent silence ruled in the air, many say.
And some of them had even the intuition
That something wrong was coming to hit terribly the nature.
What would it be? This was a pointless question for anyone
Knowing that the media did not forecast any impending- natural disaster!
Moreover, for two hundred years,
The country has experienced only violent cyclones
That had been all predicted.
Always was that a cry of alarm raised all people's awareness
Of the approaching disaster.
For usually they had the population evacuate any place
That is exposed to riparian pressures.
Always was that they were warned against torrential streams
That usually ravaged the plains and took away crops and livestock.
In short, everyone's attention had been focused on floods
Due to the serious damages the population underwent
From the swollen rivers since long ago!

In addition, it was believed that in case of natural disasters,
A mansion in this country was a safer place than a frail home.
However, only by an evening,
A fierce earthquake sprang and changed that conception immediately!
An important number of large buildings collapsed,
Which claimed so many human lives!
The deadly catastrophe transformed palaces into unprecedented killing fields.
It changed churches into ruins
Where they scavenged the remains of worshippers
Whom the great carnage unexpectedly caught!
This disaster changed schools into mounds of debris
That covered teachers' and learners' bodies like a common grave.

Just a while ago, however, everything had seemed to be normal this
Tuesday!
The whole entire Port-au -Prince had been working as usually.
No one could figure out how so quickly, I mean, within thirty seconds
only,
It had changed into a vale of tears, a pitiable cemetery, or a kind of a
battlefield
What a pity, in a so short time!

The disaster victimized people of all sorts: men, women and children!
The streams of blood flowed under the rubbles of the collapsed houses
Whence thousand survivors rushed desperately into the roads,
Carrying their wounded or their dear dead ones,
And vociferously imploring the help of the heaven!

Port - au- Prince crushed, no need to say
That the toll of casualties was so heavy at Turgeau too!
And the neighbors of the Trazileo, in delirium, had seen the villa collapse
And had therefore, concluded that inevitably
Joshua and Linda should have died
What about the children who are physically more vulnerable!
Since of the castle no wall remained standing,
Nor any post regardless of their size.
The disaster had torn apart everything!
Therefore the Trazileo seemed to perish for real!

CHAPTER FORTY-FIVE

They Had Got It Wrong!

The neighbors had made a hasty conclusion about the Trazileo family.
Of the building that seemed to be crushed
One part remained underneath without breaking.
It had sunk down and held all of them captive, frantic, hopeless,
Cut off from the outside, and barely breathing,
Resigned to death after so many unsuccessful attempts
To ascend from the hole in which it was so dark!

Linda on her part, tired of fighting, relied on God only.
She tried to urge the Almighty God to save her and her family without delay!
This is the first time she prayed her heavenly Father so fervently!
What a plea in that woe time she made for their survival!
As follows she uttered her supplications:

"O God of the universe, if you take us out of this place
That will become soon our grave,
I will sacrifice to you alone, I swear, the rest of my life!
May you hear my prayer and take pity on us
As I have been desperately crying for help for hours!
Ah, Great God, could you remember our buried-living souls!
I know, your arms, O Lord, are not too short
To remove us from here and prolong God our life!
To bring out of here, Father, our buried souls
While the dreadful death constantly frightens us!

O you who had heard all the prayer of Jonas,
May you send us a hand!
A hand which you will strengthen to break these barriers!
To hammer down these rocks and these gigantic walls!
Take off these doors and break all these irons
That retain all of us here, soon our last dwelling!

For, you alone, great God!
You alone know how we pine after our rescue!
You alone, see us here, unique- loving God,
You alone, you see us dying under the debris,
You alone, see us inert under the columns!
You alone, you watch our crushed-bleeding-moaning heart,
As under this dust, we are losing our whole breath!
Make it happen, O God, that my so weak voice
Passes through these barriers and reaches one outside!
Before we extinguish powerless in this place!

You who always set free your people on earth
By breaking all ramparts which held him captive,
Those people, whom you chose despite their transgressions,
Those people who failed to venerate you, great God!
Today may you listen to your so poor servant!
As constantly besieged and resigned to death
She lies in this abyss cut off from the sunlight!

O Great God, Jehovah, condescend to save us
As you rescued Daniel from the cruel lions' jaws
Which the impious ones assigned for his execution!
May you, God, rescue us like the three young Hebrews
Whom you set free and safe out of the furnace
When they had to choose in their so great dilemma
To die loyal to you in the burning fire!

Could we see act for us, God, your holy finger
That once tore down all the walls of Jericho!
So that in that great day without fight they fell
So many enemies of your people Great God!
May that finger that dried the streams of the Red Sea,
Intervene for our lives today Almighty Lord,
And pave a way to us and free us like sometime
When you brought your people out of Babylon!
Oh! Take pity on us! And let all my request
In the name of your son ascend to you, O Lord,

Go up from this hiding where yearning for your help
I desperately see my people close to death
On this January 12, the first month of the year!
When that ordeal caught us and caused us to be here!

But if it's that your will that we all remain here
And close our tired eyes for the ultimate sleep,
Oh! Let my desire yield to your decision!
Oh! If that is your will, could you remember us!
At the appointed day for your Son to wake up
All those staying in rest in the great sleep of death
And then you will destroy our greatest enemy[114].

---

[114]   Death is our greatest enemy.

CHAPTER FORTY-SIX

In the Quarter of Bel-Air

In Bel-Air[115] as well, the specter of death had left countless dead bodies.
Regardless of their social background, their level of wealth, or their age,
Young and old, poor and wealthy, good and less good ones,
It struck all of them in its deadly crusade.

And its blind passage was so terrifying
That of the Church, alas, the ruling class partly
Underwent the same destruction as the flock fallen in full adoration
When the cathedral, in fact, collapsed
Claiming the lives of those whom the worship gathered
Under this vault witness of so many stories
And of so glorious facts, worthy of memory!
It was disappointing for so many people!

---

[115]   The first quarter of Port-au-Prince.

CHAPTER FORTY-SEVEN

A Call to Action

Meanwhile, sad Theodore, like so many fellows,
Did all what a true apostle of Christ would have done.
He inquired into his brothers' situation,
By keeping eye on them through the whole neighborhood!
He braved the appalling spectacle of blood
That streamed from underneath the countless corpses!
In few words, he truly cared for these
Whom he as a shepherd, he had then in his charge!
Of course, with all his peers he assisted all the fold
That faced up to and dealt with a terrible loss,
A loss that put, alas, everyone on mourning:
Sister Marilia, what a pity, had died!
She had been a servant well known for her virtue.
Hence, her death caused a general outpouring
As soon as she was deemed dead in that tragedy!
Oh! What a heavy task for the beloved Theo
Due to the grief of so many within his herd
Who distraughtly bewailed over the departure
Of their loved ones and so many others as wells!
He had to fly to help people in agony!
He had to fly and save many dejected souls
Who lay motionless on the brink of extinction!
Under the rubbles, or wherever they were found!
Moreover, of many he still ignored the state
While he felt himself brokenhearted for all
And particularly for the young "brother," Jain
Who always seemed to be his favorite-good friend!

Theodore had to commiserate with Jain
Since this little brother desperately assumed
That his mother Linda hopelessly passed away!
Theo tried to console him in that circumstance
By imploring for him the love of the True God!
Then, through a prayer said with soothing words and charms,
He managed to appease the tearful -young brother.
He succeeded in having the latter calm down
Despite uproar, tumult, strident cries everywhere
All dwellers had that mourn in sharing!
Soon after Theodore had prayed for brother Jain,
The former could not help in spite of his great strength
Bursting into tears too! Then a counterpart
Proposed Theo to form a strong rescuing team
That had to accomplish some courageous actions!
Jain in that circumstance would be the first to be served.
And he will prove to be so grateful for that!

CHAPTER FORTY-EIGHT

They Got Ready

The proposal met everyone's agreement.
It consisted of organizing quickly a relief group
In favor of those who needed assistance and care in that circumstance.
Then twenty – eight males and females, motivated by altruism,
Volunteered to tackle together any manly tasks
That meant to snatch from death whomever they could in that particular time.
But they should target anyone among their people first.
Therefore it took them an advisor,
Someone to pass urgent instructions when necessary
And to show them how to do things rapidly and safely;
Brother Theo himself assumed this great role.
For he used to keep everything under control
When violent storms stroke his congregation
And left everyone with endless fear and concerns!
Below are listed the names of the team makers:

Alcibiade Zephir, Adrien Odonel,
Agenor Jolius, Semexant Ducarmel,
Jean-Robert Mcadolphe, Andre Marc-Similien
Saintcyr Jean Sainvilus, Nicolas Parisien,
Agéta Renelus, Mariette Angelus
Jean-David Jolibois, Clement-Pierre Romélus
Sidonie Dorélus, Nasson Jean Marc-Aurèle,
Hilenfant Saint-hilaire, Iphigenie Adele,
Saurel Anacreon, Degazon Martineau,
Lorémond Jean -Valcourt, Balthazar Mirabeau,
Josie Derenoncour, Sonia Marie- Josiane,
Jackerbie Salomon, Marie -Josie Villane,
Jean -Michel Raphael, Marc- Antoine Agenor
Solon, Paul -Dumarsais, and Juste Theodore.

The group included people with multiple skills.
It involved nurses, plumbers, engineers
Members who were good in taming stone and iron!
Volunteers who could make a breach and dig a pit!
It relied on swimmers tireless in flood time.
There were also among them excellent axmen
To crack down some any gigantic poles
What about to set free anyone
Who would be trapped under the fallen roofs?
And all they could deal with the disconsolate ones
Of whom many distraughtly were weeping
For finding themselves to be either legless cripple,
Or one-legged, or one-eye, or blind
As they worry about knowing how many dear ones they had lost
Or whether they still had some hope in the existence.

And our twenty-four merciful heroes
Brought with themselves saws, hammers, and strings
Flashes and batteries and one generator which
They might use at a certain time,
Because shortly darkness would be about to come
And sadden some more the bereaved areas.
They took also with them gloves, shovels, and machetes,
And pickaxes and two longer scales.

In terms of tools, in fact, they had everything,
Everything needed anywhere their spirit of sacrifice would lead them.
First care kits, and oxygen pump
Theodore foresaw all of them as a good guide,
Not to mention that he did carry some stretchers in hope
That they would use them soon!
And as for sheets and warm dresses, he also wore some too.
He did not forget about water and food
For he believed that they were going out for long!
But prior to doing anything,
He said a prayer to ask our divine Father for help.

CHAPTER FORTY-NINE

Rescue

Jain getting involved in this undertaking felt appeased little by little.
He got strengthened after he heard that prayer.
In fact, this supplication reminded him
That in case his mother would have passed away, he would see her again
Like so many people sleeping in death, but at her appointed day.
It would be a huge mistake on Theodore's part
If praying with all heart he failed to say those words
To calm Jain down by reminding him
That the previous disaster was not planned by our Divine Father
And that our loving God is looking forward to ending our plagues
And our calamities which Satan and his demons have caused.

Happily, Theodore's prayer reminded Jain
That God will destroy all these bad things through the battle of
Armageddon.
Those sacred words had a relief effect on Jain's spirit
Since he had been waiting for the Kingdom of God
Which he knew to be the only one powerful government
That can annihilate our pains, our sorrows, and our tribulations!
Oh! How wise Brother Theo was when saying those things in his prayers
To prepare Jain to accept anything might happen to Linda!

And shortly after, our brave men were there,
I mean, at the premises of the collapsed villa which Jain had shown them.
"Let us set to work now!" Theodore exclaimed,
Like a general attacking a fortress.
At that time, all the team members hurried up to work
Hoping like the fishermen to find anything:
A living person, a dead body, or half-dead and so on!
In the meantime, Jain silently prayed, prayed, and prayed very hard!
A few minutes after, they found Joshua who was breathing hardly.
Oh! How wounded he was!

Few seconds later, Linda was found who remained attached to a table.
She almost stopped breathing.
She was bleeding at her shoulders and got her legs broken.
And next to her were found her two boys lying on their dinners.
They were in serious condition.
So was the whole family pulled away from death!
As for the maid, she was not found there.
For during the earthquake, she had been safe and sound outside.
The rescue operation lasted two hours.
There was no one else hurt in the ruined abode.

Then, under the supervision of Jain,
The Trazileo were transported to the neighboring hospital.
It was late, however, the medical team worked like in the daytime.
They managed to save these lives rapidly.
Apparently, as said in these lines,
In that moment, there was no a break at this medical setting in Canapé
Vert!
And since then, Theodore will do his best
So the Trazileo family could receive from other "brothers" a very close
attention.
But because he had other places to go,
Just after he put all these four out of the danger,
He and all his brave men got to other locations
To rescue other victims on the verge of death!

CHAPTER FIFTY

The Funeral of Marília

Since the earthquake, Theodore couldn't help shedding tears.
Oh, how pitiful he was!
He had seen too many sickening things happen!
And maybe, if he did not pray to God a lot,
He would lack the courage which he needed to endorse everything.
Particularly, he would fail to remain a fortifying heart even for his own family
While having many people to console!
For at that time, he had to keep hopeful those who felt down!
He had to comfort all those who had the blues for their own future
As long as they went across this ordeal!
He had to cheer up so many
Who were either plunging into distress or overcome by an excruciating pain!
Happily, in time of trials,
The true God always provides his people with a good guide
Or with a beloved one to be as blameless as Theodore!

However, Brother Theo still awaited more sad-oncoming events.
And particularly, he waited for the worst moment of these trials:
The funeral of Sister Marilia!
Since the catastrophe, her corpse had been taken to the funeral home.
In that circumstance, one of the embalmers came to hate his profession.
"For the first time in my life," he said,
"I have seen too many dead bodies in the morgue!
Oh, how such a calamity has stricken us so cruelly!"

By the time, Theodore at the funeral pumps remained speechless.
For the hour which he dreaded so much was well arriving.
It was 10 o'clock A.M, and the whole mournful assembly flocked to the mortuary.
Of all Marilia's friends, Jain was the only one to miss her funeral.

Of course, since the rescue of the Trazileo,
Jain had volunteered to stay at their bedsides.
That's why he came to be a key player in all their affairs.
So against his wishes Jain was absent from the funeral home
That is located a little near the burial place.
In a while later, the defunct sister was about to be inhumed there in her own grave.
Years ago she had built this tomb after her husband had died.

In the grieving hall, brothers, sisters, friends and other sympathizers
Lined up and marched by the side of the coffin
Prior to taking a seat and listening to a funeral talk
That Brother Gilbert was ready to give.
Brother Gilbert was among these who safely came out of the earthquake.
Without a shadow of doubt,
This orator had known the defunct sister since she was a child.
Like Theodore, he did all he could to encourage his neighbors at that critical time.

And the deceased sister lying in her coffin like in her bed,
Was dressed in her most sumptuous attire!
To tell the truth, without this mournful atmosphere,
Without the coffin, and without endless groans caused by this loss,
Sister Marilia through her embalmed face and her hairstyle
Would not look like a dead body!
She would be of course similar to the pretty woman
Who she had been at her wedding day!

But according to a French saying, when the wine is drawn, it must be drunk.
Meaning, despite that universal bereavement
Everyone had to stay powerless
And accept that the cruel accident had indeed claimed the life of Sister Marilia!
No matter how she was good!
In reality, death awaits every living soul
Without wondering whether one is a king, a prince, a lord,
An honest person, or a wrongdoer!

Then came the moment to shut the coffin;
On the faces sank the largest river of tears.
Yet did Theodore control himself and started with the song *"endless life"*.
After that, the speaker Gilbert went up the stage
In front of an audience at the peak of sadness!

CHAPTER FIFTY-ONE

Thus Spoke the Orator

"Upon seeing our gathering in this hall this morning,"
Gilbert said, as they uttered shrill cries,
"There is no doubt that in this nefarious moment,
We have come here to perform an ultimate duty in behalf of Sister Marilia
Whom we have so terribly missed during the devastating earthquake!
Today, it's evident that her funeral has destroyed our joy!
And we don't know for how long we will be deprived of our happiness
As shows this sonorous room in which, currently,
We hear weary- lugubrious moans commingle laments,
Sighs of sympathy and affliction!
As show all these powerful dins,
These explosions of tantrums and these torrents of tears!

Well! We understand you, Dear parents and friends,
Whom her departure afflicts,
We understand the reasons of your distress!
We understand why this dismay has taken over your mind
On this gloomy morning
When even the sun has stopped from shining with its supreme brilliance!
That's why I beg you in spite of your legitimate tears
To recall today who Sister Marilia was!
And allow me, please, to tell you what her tastes, her goal and her hope
in life were!
And how come she finally entered this silence four days ago!

And we are going to investigate together into the sleep of death
That has caused so many harms to us!
Then, we will be able to reflect on Marilia's footsteps
And see how she had been able to acquire a place in God's memory
For the eternal life
When the Earth becomes new soon!

In fact, who was Sister Marilia?

This morning, this question deserves our full attention.

Everyone knows how she has done a commendable reputation with all of us here,

And how proud we feel whenever we mention her name!

Born in Croix des Bouquets in nineteen - hundred and fifty,

She was the unique child of her mother, Mary Lucie with her father, John.

And in this family, she was spoiled as the one offspring and unique daughter

And there she led a happy existence until she got married with Mr. David Homer.

Then, she moved to her own dwelling with her husband

On Macajou Street, Port-au-Prince

Where she mothered two boys: Jean Robert and Loulou.

The latter was born as a posthumous child

Because Marilia was pregnant with this baby when, unfortunately,

Her husband died in a serious accident.

And since, she alone reared her two children up!

Very young, she was well passionate of groves:

She loved exploring the fields and the landscapes!

Today, this friend, I see her again

Who gives herself completely to the grasslands and admires the floras!

I see her smiling to the fragrant roses and to the bougainvilleas,

To the ylang ylang and to the oleander!

To all these flowers that put all souls in ecstasy!

And I imagine seeing that girl again with her infinite joy,

Listening and enjoying one by one beautiful love inspiring symphonies!

And since she became our sister

And started to follow the footsteps of the Lord next to us,

She always remained impeccable and serene!

She always cared about the perennial welfare of the congregation

In which she felt so happy and secure!

She proved to be the Rebecca, or the Sarah[116] of our time,

A servant in which love alternates with charity!

---

[116]   See Genesis 24:67

A Dorcas[117] and a generous hand
That soothed the worrying- impecunious brothers and sisters!

She was also the embodiment of the maternal love!
And she well deserved prizes and crowns
For joining the traits of a good mother with the great virtue of an exemplary wife!
This was Sister Marilia, O bereaved friends!
This was the beloved treasure which the cruel death removed from us!

In fact, what is this ugly phenomenon that subdues us to so many sufferings?
Death is simply the opposite of life.
This is the condition in which soul stops living.
When a living being stops breathing
Either following a sudden death or as the result a martyrdom
Or consequently to a long illness or otherwise,
Nothing can stop him from going to dust:
Neither incantations nor fast nor prayer
Nor the social status of which he had been proud
Nor beauty nor age nor talent
And regardless of his race or his immense fortune,
He will leave when he stops respiring,
It's over for him when comes his extinction!
Really, it's done of his soul when someone died!
As soon as his breath leaves his body!
Indeed, on earth must perish any flesh that has lost oxygen.
Without these two elements forming the mortal soul,
Here we are in the arms of the so cruel death!
Here we are making our last sigh!
Here were are, then, losing our spirit!
Then, we human souls are declared dead!
After losing a part of what made us alive in the beginning!

---

[117]   See Acts 9:36,37

And then we defunct whom everyone weeps are deposited in the last residence,
And lie unconscious and *deprived of the notion of good or bad.*[118]
For a dead one knows nothing!
And we delude ourselves if we believe
That a dead one continues existing beyond the grave,
Or if we imagine his suffering in a purgatory to wash away his sins,
Or if we think that he is undergoing a bitter punishment
In some endless- burning hell,
Or if we guess that he is admitted to paradise in eternal happiness
Far away from any allegedly suffering-damned ones!

Yes, the dead ones are unconscious,
So is Marilia whom the cruel disaster struck three days ago!
This is the situation of our compatriots who are gone too!
All of them being mown down by the wicked death,
They no longer know nothing and return to their soil!

Yet, God promised that from their tomb
He will rescue those who are entered wherever they had expired:
No matter whether they perished at the bottom of an ocean
Or in the embers of a volcano!
No matter whether their corpses were not found,
They will return one day at the call of Jesus the conqueror of death!

Then, death will no longer harm to us humans!
Then, they will come back as they were! Without any change in their personality
So that people can recognize them as a son recognizes his father, or his ancestor,
A father his child, a girl her mother!
Thus, the Christ will make their return take place.
That was Marilia's hope, bereft friends,
A hope that she constantly proclaimed everywhere!

---

[118]   See Ecclesiastes 9:5,10

Marilia had always likened death to a sleep
That should end by the revival of those whom
Jesus will recall from the nothingness
After he replaces our wicked world by the new-promised one!
And since the Bible can never lie·
We remain certain that our Sister Marilia will come back.

Yes, she will come back soon!
From the places in which rest they that in their sleep no longer admire the roses!
She will come back soon!
As if nothing had happened, so she can enjoy the prospect of living forever!
She will come back soon!
As did Lazarus, without any mental and physical damages!
Then, we will experience the real happiness
Without anymore fear of death and with serenity!

Thus while mourning her departure today,
Let us be so comforted by this powerful hope!
Let us now remember that our grief is about to slip away!
And that, tomorrow, joy we will have to find soon under the eyes of the true God!
For He has sworn it by himself!
He has promised the definitive remedy to our overwhelming evil!
This evil that may spread, alas, its spectrum at every moment!

But now that in such a sleep she lies unaware of everything
And even of her condition,
Should not her experience move us to reflect on our own existence?
That's why today we all are invited
To think of our good relations with our great God Jehovah!
For before He establishes on earth his Kingdom,
He would certainly keep us alive in His memory
In case our history might end too[119] any time!

---

[119]   See Ecclesiastes 9:11

Thus may each of us with a sincere heart pray
For the advent of His Divine Kingdom[120]
Of which forerunning sign we have already seen
With these earthquakes and others plagues[121] occurring everywhere today!
Let us be consoled, for the Kingdom of God will bring our salvation so soon!"

That speech had on the listeners' heart the same effect of an oasis on the desert.
The rest we will know about it, for Theodore will tell Jain of everything.

---

[120] See Revelation I:14
[121] See Mathew 24, 2 Timothy 3:1

CHAPTER FIFTY- TWO

A Regretful Mother

Linda realized how much Jain loved her.
Therefore, she felt bad for having once left him motherless.
Actually, she considered Jain being her hero!
She understood that without him,
Her people and she would have perished under the rubbles!
Seated in her wheelchair at a quiet corner,
She poured out her depressive mind as follows:

"Oh! What a shame on me, unnatural mother,
To have abandoned the son who rescued me!
What a foolish decision was mine
To deny him a care which he needed so much!
And then, I tried to hide my scandal
By leaving him alone an October morning!
And as if nothing had happened,
I thrived every day to ignore my misdeed!

"In the very time when acceding to riches
I cared very little about his sad life.
And although I well knew his missing all my love,
I stifled my conscience at the risk of his soul!
O God, I hope that you, my immortal Sovereign
Will relieve my conscience of that horrific sin!

"Oh! What a shame on me, unnatural mother,
Who got married and turned my dear son's life down!
Thus I sacrificed him to my wealthy bride groom!
When I saw my suitor fall in deep love with me,
I astutely hid him all the truth about me!
Then he, finding in me his dearest interest,
He chose me to be part of his life forever!
Quickly he married me, which I did not expect!

But I kept from telling him I had mothered a boy
Who lived with my mother in the countryside!
I refrained from disclosing to him that secret
For fear that I might kill his great passion for me!

"It's true, in that period, I looked very happy,
But in bottom of me I was in rainy days!
For as I remembered my dear-abandoned son,
I felt as if the sun never rose in my life!
And I realized as well that the Heaven someday
Would ask me for my fault before his righteous Court!
Though while enjoying my alleged success
In that circle in which I took my ascension,
I felt vain when thinking of my bad experience!

"It's true I toured the World with a loving husband!
It's true I saw other societies in the globe
And saw the lifestyle of the other nations!
In all luxurious hotels I spent wonderful days,
Tasting of the mortals the most expensive meals!
And I will not mention my very costly fares
To visit the most distant places in the earth!
But I found everything to be a vain success
For not telling the truth to lead a happy life
With my gleeful husband who just turned his thirty!

"O my God, who would say that my neglected son
Would be today the one on whom I must rely?
He who had removed me from that abyssal grave
When we were held captive in that shady basement,
All stunned by the appalling specter of death,
And having lost all hope in exiting one day!
O God, is there someone now to clean my conscience
Off this cruel remorse that silently gnaws me!
Oh! How I feel condemned in the depths of myself!
Oh! Tell me what to do, oh, my right- supreme Judge!

"Oh! What a shame on me, unnatural mother,
To deny for money the produce of my womb!
Of course, for a prestige that passes like burning stalks
When fire breaks out and destroys everything!
O God, whereas for now my son is the sole one
On whom I should rely! O God, the unique one!
Where's the splendid castle which I had loved so much?
Where's that great luxury that envied all those
Who kept coveting once our pompous lifestyle?
Where are all my hotels to which celebrities
From everywhere arrived for spending blissful days?
Where are my industries, source of windfall profits,
Which had made me crazy on a daily basis?
How many survived among my employees
Who all alongside us had arduously labored?

"Oh! What a shame on me, unnatural mother!
But whereas, now, I feel so deeply embarrassed,
I believe that my God in his so great justice
Will take pity on me and relieve my conscience!
In fact, to Him at first I owe to be alive!
Without Him, who knows, I would have lost my life!
I know that my Good God, Eternal sovereign
Can alone bring the cure to my endless sorrow!

CHAPTER FIFTY-THREE

O Mother, Calm Down!

Then, Jain came to worry about his distressed mother.
Unwittingly, he had caught her weeping in secret
And thought that he should say something to appease her!

"O Mother, could you come down? He said.
Your suffering, I know, has been extremely cruel!
But despite everything, I would like you
To see your situation with a positive eye!
Do you know how at the edge of your last moment
You were snatched from the grave?
Do you know how many saved you from that mishap?
O Mom, how many died in that day while you are alive?

I know, you are going through the hardest time in your life.
However, don't you realize that across your trials
The good heaven has saved my two arms to help you?
And haven't you seen me always at your bedside
Trying to drive your grief away?
O Mom, please, dry your tears.
Pluck up your courage and trust in God, who alone
Can heal you soon and have you forget everything."

"My son, my son, my son, Linda said, O my son,
How can I be strong across those woes today?
It's true! You have supported me throughout my cruel time!
It is true! God has preserved you in order to assist me!
And woe to me, if I had the cheek to ignore
All the sacrifices which you have made for me!
However, I also know that I should swallow that cup
For having abandoned you so early in your life!"

"O Mom, spare me these negative words, please!
For they greatly dishonor the name of our merciful God
And blame on Him all our sufferings.
When a calamity strikes us, we shouldn't hold God responsible for it.
In fact, even though He has witnessed all our sins,
Far away from Him to chastise us with the evil!

"O Mom, could you stop feeling bad about me?
Really, there is no link between those atrocities
And the fact that you neglected me as a child!
If God wanted to punish you that way,
Why wouldn't He let you die in the basement?
And why would He send a team to rescue you?

O Mother, don't you see how blessed you had been in that day
To be found alive under the rubbles?
Of course, when you'd tour the city a while,
You would meet countless bereaved ones mourning barely identifiable
bodies
To be put into the mass graves!
What were the names of those the victims? Jean? Pierre? Durosier?
They were so numberless that they piled up like a dune,
All united in death: men and women,
Parents and children, singles and married couples, and so on!
All of them then lying within the dust,
So was *"the evil which spreads out the terror[122]"*
About which Jean de La Fontaine had talked!
Lucretius also spoke of a plague having claimed many lives in Athens!
Homer in its Iliad also celebrated the striking loss of countless victims
Whom Apollo would have killed for the sake of his humiliated prophet!
Voltaire as well grieved the death of countless victims of Lisbon disaster!
Real or legendary, these accounts remain just written stories.

---

[122] In *"Les Animaux Maladies de la Peste"*.

But what I saw as a teen during that dreary time
Has moved me to appreciate the greatness of God
Who prevented us from being among so many corpses!
Therefore, no matter how atrocious these events were,
We should praise the Lord for our survival.
And we should never blame on Him the deadly scourge
That might occur anywhere at any time!
For even though He allows those deplorable things to happen,
He is not the one using those things to strike us!
An earthquake occurs by a geodynamic accident,
Not by the will of our so loving God!
A earthquake happens when two tectonic plates in the depths
Break their border during their movement.
Then, under the pressure of dynamic forces,
These two disjointed blocks collide with each other,
Or go away from each other.
Hence forth, those chaos and disturbance in depths!
Then, some energy suddenly emerges and causes the ground to quiver!
Hence, those landslides, those ravages, those broken surfaces,
Those holes under the ground and these tsunamis and tides!
Those things, Mom, you already know them!"

Thus had talked Jain to his distressed mother!
But he failed to quiet her down.
She still wanted to know the reason why God allows evil on earth.

CHAPTER FIFTY-FOUR

No Hope for us?

"O Son, how proud I am of you!
With a timorous heart you really stand up for God!
Me too, I am fearful of God,
Yet do I speak negatively across my trials.
In fact, when I think about the current situation,
I have the feeling that God forgets about our planet exposed to all dangers:
Hurricanes, tornadoes, floods, earthquake and so on!
And I deplore the fact that I can't talk to God face to face
To ask Him why He has condoned so many atrocities on earth
Whence, however, we raised our endless prayers to his eternal throne!
Does not He see our going through all of those disasters?
Once, Haiti was hit. So was the Japan later.
And who knows where in our planet will spring another mishap?

"No one is safe in any continents!
Worse yet has been predicted the immersion of some areas anytime.
Why has not a loving and all-powerful God averted these dangers off the earth?
He who has shown his peerless wisdom by creating that beautiful planet,
How come he has let it be the unique-imperiled one in the cosmic world?
Why should we always dread a heartbreaking catastrophe?
Is not the terrestrial globe a tiny point
Among the legions of orbits swarming the space?
Is not the sun's size one million times larger than the earth's?
And as regards the Milky Way or solar system
Do not its countless stars operate safely with the exception of the earth?
We could make the same observation
About immeasurable clusters of galaxies placed under the laws of gravitation!
Please, answer these questions if you can, Son.
For I feel bewildered when I realize
That earth is the only one planet having escaped the attention of the Creator!"

"O, Mom, should we blame on God the fact that
Earth has been exposed to all disasters? Jain asked.
I am telling you, if there were any insignificant negligence in God,
Our situation would be worst!
In fact, let's think about what would happen
If God had placed the sun or the moon a little closer to the earth!
Undoubtedly, we would become lifeless like the rocks!

"What would happen all of a sudden if the Author of life
Cut off the oxygen for a while?
All human and animal species would perish for sure!
And how would be life possible on earth if He did not provide water in abundance?
All living things would die down here!
Indeed, on those factors depends our existence.
And what about the cycles which He has established?
Without these changes,
Our very existence would be subjected to worse hassles.

Imagine, Mom, how boring life would be
If He did not create summer to succeed to spring,
And fall to summer, and winter to fall!
In the fields, all things would be affected.
And our condition would be fatal if God did not change water into vapor.
For the sea itself, storing too much water would submerge the cities!
And without this vapor that rises from the sea, there would be no precipitation.
Consequently, drought would be everywhere
Harming to plants, to animals and to humans!
All those positive things are the result of infallible laws
Which the true God made for our happiness,
On a perfect earth that, however, proves to be the theatre of tear-jerking woes!

All things considered, it is in our hands that this globe has deteriorated.
God had created it for the happiness of the human species,

Who unhappily far from appreciating it, has changed it into a hideous dwelling!
Men have behaved as a bad beneficiary of the inhabited earth;
That is the source of the problems.
Hence, come all our sufferings and deadly plagues!
To fill their egoistic desires,
Men have thought that it is quite normal to break that gift
By crossing the lines imposed by the divine laws.
Consequently, earth has been exhausted.
No need, in fact, of a complicated speech to explain it
To whoever needs to understand it!
It's like a machine that we buy and whose manual we ignore!
Failure to observing the handbook's instructions
To properly use the appliance will result in its breakdown very soon!
In his event, no matter how expensive the instrument is,
It should be out of use.

Similarly, men have been a bad tenant on the inhabited earth
For ignoring its laws!
These who care a few about the survival of our planet
Have tried to destroy it so many times!
In the beginning, the terrestrial globe was designed
For producing everything good to support life,
And everything good to make all species happy, worriless, sated and secure!
The birds were expected to be as jubilant
As the cheerful fishes in sweet or in salty water!
And from the hissing snake to the croaking raven,
From the jumping toad to the slow turtle,
From the domestic animals to the wild herds,
No soul would miss their joyfulness!
Could also jump with joy the mountains' goats
While the satiated- wild animals would stay in the luxuriant forests forever.
And the plants exposed to the sunlight would glow of greenery at every time
To cheer our heart up with their beauty!

"Alas, this is not what we always see today, Mom,
Since humans have trashed the earth,
Which having lost its early charms constantly calls us for help!
So the earth which God gave us humans is weeping every day!
Earth suffers from short breath and from countless sores
On the part of those who put its existence in jeopardy!
Earth is sighing as result of endless bloodsheds!
Earth keeps moaning as long as destructive battles claim human lives!
Earth cries wherever grass stops growing to remind us a place
Once ago the theatre of massacres!
And since its natural cycle of cold and heat was been interrupted,
Earth suffers from tachycardia!
With the greenhouse effect endangering its existence
Earth nearly dies suffocated by too much carbon and methane
Supplied by the modern industry!

"O Mom, even some animal species already disappeared
As others are being destroyed!
Some beasts have fled their normal dwellings
To dispute to men their livelihoods!
With quite a pace is accelerating deforestation anywhere!
Consequently, erosion changes fertile soils into barren,
Which disappoints people!

Who is at fault, O Mom, for these fatal changes?
Tell me, please, whom to blame
For the fact that earth in its hospital bed implores our compassion?
We humans are to blame, but not the loving God!
We humans who subdue the globe to our own unreal plans!
We humans who have sacked and fauna and flora!
We humans who have burnt mounts, valleys, and plains!
We humans who pollute our own environment!
We humans whose deadly weapons
Already caused two cruel- global wars
Whereas we're still lagging after real peace on earth!
We humans whose actions don't spare anybody

Not even the children who were safe once ago!
Not even the students in school and in daycare!
O Mom, what has occurred to the planet of the men?"

"Dry your tears, Son. I understand your anger!
Although lot of people blamed God for our sad existence,
As for you, you brilliantly proved his absolute innocence!
For now, I would like to know why our blameless God
Has so long turned a deaf ear to our supplications!
I would like to know why his Justice is so slow-moving
And why he allows the wicked ones to multiply our woes on earth?
How many innocent people hasn't He seen
Who were served an unjust penalty?

How many hasn't He seen who were killed defenselessly?
How many hasn't He seen who for their religious beliefs
Were uttering their last sigh on the fatal pyre?
How many has not He seen who died in the shackles of slavery?
Or who expired under the sadistic tortures by their masters?
How many questions do we have regarding His indifference to our woes?

"You're mistaken, O Mom,
If you think that God is indifferent to our ordeals, Jain Said.
In fact, you have failed to understand
That He set a time for all good people to see the evil disappear from earth.
For so soon God will destroy the author of our atrocities!
Of course, He will annihilate the power of Satan
And free our globe from his infamous domination.
Thus, the leadership of this bad angel is almost over
Knowing that our Creator will remove him from his throne
And will cast him and his demons to the abyss at the day of Armageddon!
In fact, Mom, God has allowed Satan to rule until now
To show how bad this opponent is both as a ruler
And as the originator of all our suffering on earth!

"For the present, the facts have fully proved
That we, humans, are so tired of living under Satan's domination
To collapse very soon after he and his demons get drunk of human blood
And make trouble anywhere on earth!

"Everywhere an endless crusade of death he causes!
Everywhere, discord, violence, war, racism,
And natural disasters he creates!
And he is still planning other tragedies against us
Knowing that, soon, the true God will dishonor him and his cronies
And will force them to leave!
For now, on all wise men need to wait for the great day
For our good Creator to exterminate Satan and his demons
And to open up access to the most perfect happiness on earth!

CHAPTER FIFTY-FIVE

Relief

With time flying, many have calmed down
And have adapted to the new lifestyle resulting from the disaster.
For now, a lot of people understood
How they had misconceived the source of the calamities
That may overwhelm human beings at any time.
Linda too came to know about the authentic origin
Of the catastrophes that are wrongly attributed to the Good God!
Little by little she calmed down as well!
Then, she only had one last step to make and get rid of her worry:
Declaring Jain to be her first-born son.
She will need to do so with tact
To avoid incurring her beloved spouse's wrath and disgrace!
That's why she constantly sought the favorable occasion to make her confession.

On his hand, in spite of his huge losses,
Joshua remained in his social class.
Of courses he was still a rich man!
While his neighbors on the edge of poverty grieved their painful experience,
He pitied very little about himself
And focused his attention on his household,
Which he sincerely loved!
It's been one year about since the scourge he just built a beautiful home!
Now he had something in mind:
Organizing a big party in honor of Jain, Theodore
And all others, who across that huge disaster,
Had expressed to him the love of a true apostle of Jesus
By rescuing him and his people!
In addition, he would like to become a legal foster father for Jain.
And he wanted to use all possible means to fulfill that goal.
But before doing anything, he wanted to tell his wife about his dream,
Which would offer Linda the occasion to apprise him of her eternal distress.

"What a delight for me to draw close to you, Sweetie!
O my unique friend! O wife of my misery!"
Joshua said while keeping a lustful eye on her.

"Only watching you, I can be happy!
Next to you, I forget, I forget all my worries!
Only next to you I can overcome my difficulties!
When you smile at me,
Your lavender lips make you the most beautiful woman in the world!
And then how much you take after Eve and equal her in beauty!
And by your lovely hairstyle that you should have copied from an angel's,
I am telling you, you inspire me verses like Helen to Ronsard once ago!
King Solomon would rewrite his *Book of songs*
If he had discovered your angelic face!
And what about if he had seen your white teeth similar to the falling snow!
And your love glance that attains me with its arrows?
Oh! How from dawn to night have you filled my mouth with praises!
You unmatched vine of which succulent grapes I savor everyday!
Oh! What Virginie or what Juliette inspires more ecstasy than you!"

"Oh! Blessed be the heaven! Then responds Linda,
Who has granted to my lonely soul
The most gallant and the most caressing husband on earth!
A husband who has no similar anywhere!
A husband in the arms of whom I, Linda, your beautiful- happy wife,
Quiver under love and joy intoxication!

Talk to me, my Darling! Inebriate me with love!
To you and to your affectionate words
My entire soul always pays a close attention!
Otherwise, I would be exhausted under the weight of my grief!
In your courteousness I delight so much!
Oh! How elated I am, Sweetheart!
And when you are finished transporting me to the cloud nine,
Fell free, Honey, to tell me about your little project
If you have one in your mind as you always do when you get this mood!"

"Oh! How much you know me, kind doe which I cajole!" Joshua said.
"You know when my sweet words betray a dream that appeals to me!
That's why, this morning I am opening my heart to you
On the double intention that keeps my joyful person so excited!
I can no longer resist it.
And when I should feel asleep at night, I am losing my mind!
I have vainly attempted to keep it secret.
Therefore, today I would like to unveil it to you!"

"Why did you take so long revealing that secret to me, your loving wife?
Tell me about that bee that you have in your bonnet!
Tell me all you concerns and relieve your heart, Baby!
And I should help you with anything in which you may need my support!
Look, tell me about everything! Talk to your sweetheart.

CHAPTER FIFTY-SIX

Confession

Joshua took his time to figure out which one of the two plans
He was going to reveal to Linda at first.
On her side, Linda was about to seize that occasion
To finally let him know that she is Jain's mother!
Then, the grateful husband began talking of his project.

"I am looking forward, he said, to showing to our supporters
That if we have seemed to be indifferent to their kindness,
It is far from us to forget about their intervention
To rescue us from the bottom of the debris!
In fact, my darling, whenever I think of that day,
I long for telling them how grateful we are to them
For rushing us to the hospital where they took care of us!

I thirst for giving them a reward for so many things which
They have done for us:
For providing us with a place to stay in that circumstance!
For keeping eye on us in a regular basis!
For being at our bedsides everyday!
And for making me feel so good as if nothing bad had happened!

Honey, I want to show them what kind of person I am
And that I Joshua Trazileo
Can't never ever forget about their sacrifices to support us!
It is why, on the occasion of a sumptuous party,
I'll let my satisfied soul speak to them in all respects,
Considering all that they have done and continue doing
To show their love to us with a sincere heart!

"Yes, it should be then a huge gala which
We should organize for them, o my sweet Linda,
Yes, I want to honor Brother Theodore and others

Who are among the good people still on earth!
A kind of people to listen to when coming to our doors,
They announce the joy which the Kingdom of God will bring soon down
here!"

"No decision can be wiser than yours, Honey! Linda bluntly said.
You can rely on me to make your dream come true, Baby!
I will give all my supports, Jojo, I promise!
And let us strive to work on it since today.
Now, I am waiting for you to tell me about the second project
That keeps your mind so excited in secret!"

"Thank you so much, O my beautiful wife,
For promising me your contributions with that eagerness!
Of course, I have a second dream in my mind
For an exemplary- young man whose behavior I like so much!
This is Jain your little cousin for whom I conceived quite a great design!
Because, across our ordeals, he has proved to be deeply affectionate to us
To such a degree that he deprived himself of sleep
To take care of us until we woke up!
With tears and sadness he watched our groaning
And felt life charmless in presence of our excruciating pains!

On a daily basis, he has been a kind of patient care for us
And has commingled tenderness and empathy for the sake of us
Whom he never left us unattended!
He has been there for us, Linda!
For those reasons, I dream of adopting him.
How thankful I would be to you for helping me become his father
In such a way that before Law and between our two sons
Your little cousin can receive from me
All the benefits offered by a foster father who has a certain name,
A name like the one which the Trazileo have!
Adopting this young man, that's what I want!
If you support me in this project too,
I will make you the happiest wife in the World."
At this time, Linda began her confession.

And immediately her face discloses a great worry.

"Enjoy yourself, my darling, Linda said.
And make your dream come true!
Remove from your heart all overwhelming ideas
By doing anything you can
To stay for us a joyful father as much as a happy husband
As you have always been!

"But as much as you want my happiness, Honey,
That happiness that is yours, that happiness that belongs to your children,
Allow me today, please, to uncover to you,
A secret which I have concealed for so long!
For tired of it, I feel compelled to get rid of it and have my peace back!
I will tell you about it today and end my eternal fear
Since I know that I have committed the big mistake not to tell you
About the most sickening woe which knocked on my door when I was thirteen
And that someone taking advantage of my absent parents,
Crept into my house with all the intention to humiliate me mercilessly;"

"Stop it, Dada. Please, don't come back anymore to this dark past.
You already told me what happened to you at that time.
Why should you recall that hard incident?
I never ever blamed it on you!
Listen to me, Honey,
Aren't you the most beautiful and the most faithful wife in the world?
Why would you remember a filthy assault that can't affect our wonderful love?
Put that depressing reminder aside forever!
That odious time could not prevent you
From finding in myself a beloved husband! Could it?
And it could not either block your access to our sacred bond
That shall remain intact until my death!
And what don't you have as a woman?
Has not your wedding erased the infamous scar

Left on your skin by that cursed animal having slipped into your parental home?

And considering your education and your fame,
Shouldn't you forget about that past?
Please, stop seeing yourself as the unique victim of an errant hand!
I remember you telling me it was against your will
You made such an experience in your life."
Thus, had spoken the husband!

However, despite his sympathetic words, his wife kept weeping.
"I am not done yet with my confession, Honey!
Here is the monstrous secret that I am uncovering to you today!
Please, listen to me, O Dear husband!
I need to tell you all that happened in that day:

"In fact, before I met you, the man we talk about,
Having assaulted me became the biological father of my first child!
That's what I managed to keep into hiding.
Today, I implore your forgiveness for keeping it secret!
And I rely on your clemency to be happy!
And I wish you could remain as good as you have always been for me!"

"O God, why am I not an astronaut? Joshua asked.
After that cruel surprise,
I would beat a hasty retreat to another planet!
Why am I not an astronaut, O God!
I'd go hide myself far away from the earth
Until you cure my bleeding wound!
Ah! Linda, I could hardly deal with the fact
That you had been abused so early!
Since you apprised me of that incident,
Love, compassion, jealousy, vengeance
Have filled my heart for the sake of yourself!
However, today I can't accept that you also got your first baby from that attack!
I am tired of that, Madam!"

"I know it as well, O my husband, Linda said!
I know that you are tired of it.
And if should discharge your anger at me,
Remember that I am the mother of your children!
Remember us, in Africa, and in Venice!
Remember the loyalty that I have promised you!
Remind of the infinite tenderness having featured our bond!
And deign to flex your legitimate wrath
And absolve me of the evil that victimized you!
Be merciful to me, I live only for you!
Please, calm down and condone the fault of your servant!"

"I know you! Joshua said. Now, you try to touch me!
But it will take time before I can forget your silence about your first child.
Where is your son? How old is he?
Where did you raise him? Does he live in this city?
What school does he attend? How does he consider me?
How does he look like?
Tell me, Linda, how he sees his half brothers.
Will he love them sincerely?"
"Honey, don't worry that much about this young man. Linda said.
He knows you already as his father!
And since he was a little boy, you have known him
In such a way that you have admired him!"

"Ha ha ha! I have known your son since he was little!
To the point that I have admired him you said!
Are you crazy, Linda! Joshua exclaims."

"You already know him and love him as well, Linda continued.
And he delights in your presence and sees in his half- brothers his own blood
And the blessed offspring of his dear mother!
He loves them so much and already proves to be their benefactor!
A heart that transcends himself at the time of peril
To save them from the lion's jaw!
Basically, if I feel sorry

For covering the parenthood links between him and me!
I am so proud, however, to have such a son!
For if he did not exist, maybe should have we all perished under the rubbles!
If he were not alive, maybe even Theodore and his good team
Would fail to remove us from the death's teeth!
That' why, I have an advice for all the abused mothers
Who received a baby from a barefoot father!
Oh! Could you take good care of the child of your womb,
Who may in the future serve a good purpose!
If pregnant you become after you were abused,
O friends, teach your child how to obey the loving God!
Remember that your child has a Father in heaven to protect him.
Thus undertake to leave him alive in your stomach."

At this time, Linda bemoaning her bad experience uttered a strident noise!
Then, Joshua with a more tender voice tried to calm her down as follows:
"Tell me the name of your son, O Madam,
Instead of saddening me anymore!
Tell me well who he is if you're really seeking my forgiveness today!"

"At that time, Linda all sad looked throughout the park, where took place this scene.
And then, she said: Jain is he!"

"Alas! My God, alas!
What have I done today? Joshua soliloquized.
If I knew you were talking in behalf of Jain,
I would surely hold my tongue already!
Honey, I know that we all owe Jain our lives!
Forgive my mistakes, forgive my madness, Sweetie,
Forgive, please, my stupid question relating to the integrity of your so good boy!
Let's go, Linda, let's go, let's go to the lawyer.
Let's go and make Jain my heir
And you, you'll remain forever my sole and unique Linda
And the woman of my heart!

And we will delight in the honey of our love everyday!
Hence, all the poets will always speak about us!"

At these words, weeping Linda forgot her distress
And with a unrivaled tenderness,
She threw herself into her husband's lap.
One kiss, two kisses, and twenty-one kisses she madly gave him!
Since then, she was no longer sad.

End

Printed in the United States
By Bookmasters